COOLHAUS
ICE CREAM BOOK

**NATASHA CASE &
FREYA ESTRELLER**

with Kathleen Squires

Photographs by Brian Leatart | Location Photographs by Penny De Los Santos
Illustrations by Design, Bitches

A RUX MARTIN BOOK
HOUGHTON MIFFLIN HARCOURT
BOSTON   NEW YORK   2014

Copyright © 2014 by Farchitecture BB, LLC F/S/O
Food photographs © Brian Leatart
Location photographs © Penny De Los Santos
Illustrations © Design, Bitches

For information about permission to reproduce selections from this
book, write to Permissions, Houghton Mifflin Harcourt Publishing
Company, 215 Park Avenue South, New York, New York 10003.

www.hmhco.com

Library of Congress Cataloging-in-Publication Data
Case, Natasha.
   The coolhaus cookbook : custom-built sandwiches
with crazy-good combos of cookies, ice creams,
gelatos & sorbets / Natasha Case & Freya Estreller ;
with Kathleen Squires ; photographs by Brian Leatart,
location photographs by Penny De Los Santos ;
illustrations by Design, Bitches.
        pages cm
   "A Rux Martin book."
   ISBN 978-0-544-12004-4 (cloth); 978-0-544-12978-8 (ebk)
1. Ice cream sandwiches. 2. Cookies. I. Estreller, Freya.
II. Squires, Kathleen. III. Title.
   TX796.I45C38 2014
   641.86'54—dc23
                         2013021735

Book design by Laura Palese
Food styling by Liesl Maggiore
Prop styling by Amy Paliwoda

Printed in China
SCP 10 9 8 7 6 5 4 3 2 1

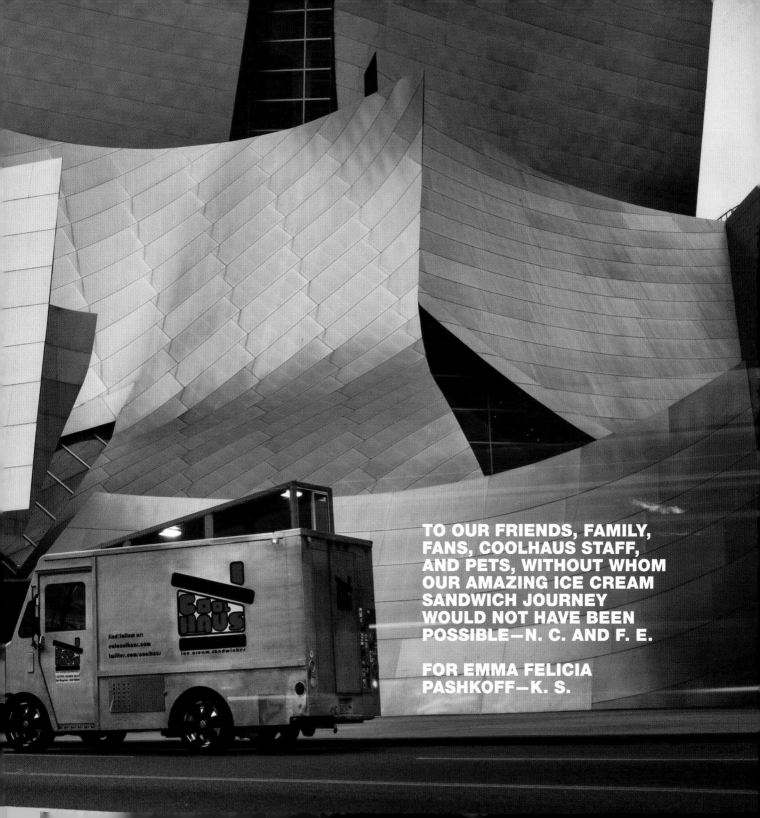

TO OUR FRIENDS, FAMILY,
FANS, COOLHAUS STAFF,
AND PETS, WITHOUT WHOM
OUR AMAZING ICE CREAM
SANDWICH JOURNEY
WOULD NOT HAVE BEEN
POSSIBLE—N. C. AND F. E.

FOR EMMA FELICIA
PASHKOFF—K. S.

CONTENTS

OUR
ARCHITECTURAL
ICE CREAM
SANDWICHES

COOKIE +	ICE CREAM =	SANDWICH
Snickerdoodle	Cookies & Sweet Cream	Peter Cook-ies and Cream (page 36)
Chocolate Chip	Dirty Mint Chip	Buck-mint-ster Fuller (page 40)
Chocolate Chip	Tahitian Vanilla Bean	Mies Vanilla der Rohe (page 42)
Double Chocolate	Dirty Mint Chip	Mint-imalism (page 40)
Oatmeal Raisin	Baked Apple	Renzo Apple Pie-ano (page 48)
Snickerdoodle	Key Lime Pie	Highlime Pie (page 53)
Double Chocolate	Bananas Foster	Bananas Norman Foster (page 61)
Oatmeal Raisin	Balsamic Fig Mascarpone	Eric Owen Moss-carpone (page 95)
S'mores	Nutella Toasted Almond	David Rocky Roadwell (page 101)
Double Chocolate	Peanut Butter	I. M. Pei-nut Butter (page 103)
Snickerdoodle	Salted Caramel	Caramia Lehrer (page 109)
Gluten-Free Coconut Almond Chocolate Chip	Salted Chocolate Almond Joy	Jennifer's Joy (page 112)
Chocolate Chip	Brown Butter Candied Bacon	Louis Ba-kahn (page 126)
Red Velvet	Coffee Oreo	Oreo Heckman (page 134)
Snickerdoodle	Earl Grey	Le Corbus-tea-er (page 136)
Vegan Ginger Molasses	Green Tea	Tea-dao Ando (page 139)
Vegan Ginger Molasses	Meyer Lemon Gelato	Richard Meyer Lemon (page 156)
Snickerdoodle	Strawberries & Cream Gelato	Frank Behry (page 160)
Vegan Ginger Molasses	Blood Orange Sorbet	Orange Julius Shulman (page 170)
Vegan Ginger Molasses	Mango Sorbet	Thom Mayne-go (page 174)
Snickerdoodle	Gin & Tonic Sorbet	Gin & Arquitec-tonic-a (page 178)

INTRODUCTION

All the cool kids in school had junk food. They always had a good stash of sweets, like Gummi Bears or Nerds. We had hopelessly dull health food or eccentric ethnic food. Our homes were not super-popular for playdates with kids looking for good after-school snacks.

So we're not going to start this cookbook off by waxing nostalgic on how our families inspired our culinary journeys. There won't be tales of a pint-size Natasha licking the spoon just out of Mom's mixing bowl. Or recollections from Freya of comforting oven aromas pervading her northeast L.A. home. In fact, Coolhaus may have been a backlash to our nonculinary upbringings, which were (probably wisely) spent outside of the kitchen.

Today, when we bring flavors like Fried Chicken & Waffle into our parents' homes, they wonder, *Where did this all come from?* Yet they proudly make space in their freezers for packs of Mint-imalism sandwiches—refreshing Dirty Mint Chip Ice Cream wedged between two fudgy Double Chocolate Cookies—or pints of our salty, sweet, rich, and velvety Brown Butter Candied Bacon. To us, that feels just as good as the days when they would tack our A+ homework on the refrigerator door.

PITREAL

UR SHOP:
n Blvd.
90232

COOLHAUS MENU

ONE STORY ICE CREAM SANDWICH	$6
TWO STORY ICE CREAM SANDWICH	$10
ONE SCOOP IN A CUP	$4
TWO SCOOPS IN A CUP	$7
PINT OF ICE CREAM	$12
ONE COOKIE	$2
THREE COOKIES	$5
BAKER'S DOZEN COOKIES	$12
ICE CREAM SANDWICH SKYSCRAPER	$25
BOTTLED WATER	$2
POPSICLE	$2

WE HEART YOU COACHELLA

WHOLE FOODS

Give a Coolhaus kudo from your mobile

follow, find or request us at:
www.twitter.com/
Coolhaus LA
www.eatcoolhaus.com

MEET NATASHA (RIGHT)

To Natasha's architect dad, French cooking meant making coq au vin and drinking the extra wine while stirring the pot. Her mom, a cartoon animator, was a Berkeley-bred vegetarian. Health food ruled. Lunch was a brown paper bag with a banana on the bottom, a fruit cup, and a natural–peanut butter sandwich (no jelly allowed) or tuna with no mayo and frighteningly dark green lettuce. Definitely not tradable commodities in the school lunchroom.

Natasha's experience making desserts as a child extended to opening a box of brownie mix, stirring in oil and eggs, placing it in the oven . . . and forgetting all about it as she trotted off to soccer practice. (Her parents came home to a smoke-filled kitchen.)

Desserts in her household were low-fat ice creams and uncool birthday carrot cakes. She is still grateful for a trip to the East Coast to visit relatives, during which she was introduced to her first full-fat ice cream—a life-changing experience.

In college, Natasha's close friend Justine taught her that decadent desserts weren't just bought in elegant pastry shops; they could actually be whipped up at home. Justine thought nothing of making an iced three-layer cake to reward her boyfriend for doing well on a math exam. From then on, butterfat found a permanent place in Natasha's consciousness.

Today, not a day goes by when she's not surrounded by incredible flavors like Salted Chocolate or Froot Loops and Milk.

MEET FREYA (LEFT)

Freya's childhood meals were a mishmash of her Filipino and Chinese heritage. She could always count on rice being in the rice cooker. While Freya embraced the cuisine of her heritage, she sometimes wanted fried chicken or pizza. Instead, pig's-blood and offal stew, called *dinuguan*, or boiled duck fetus, known as *balut*, were often on the dinner table. Desserts were gelatinous affairs like *halo halo*, a mix of ice cream, shaved ice, red beans, coconut gelatin cubes, and a plethora of assorted artificial ingredients, and *puto*, a wiggly rice cake that doesn't taste like much of anything. Or her dad's inventions, things like mashed-up avocado with milk, sugar, and creamed corn.

Freya remembers her first salty chocolate chip cookie as a turning point, making her think, *Why can't every dessert be like this?* In a new quest of mixing the savory and the sweet, she found herself at a young age creating her own ice cream sandwiches by putting a block of Neapolitan ice cream between two slices of Wonder Bread. Today, her savory palate has been the driving force behind ice cream flavors such as the luxurious Peking Duck and tangy, sweet-and-sour Balsamic Fig Mascarpone.

HOW ICE CREAM SANDWICHES SAVED OUR CAREERS

Not to throw our families under the bus—quite the contrary. For Natasha, the denial of the most basic edible childhood pleasures fueled her drive to become an expert in the field of sweets. And the exotic flavors of Freya's upbringing primed her palate for some of Coolhaus's best, and most experimental, flavors. Our architecturally inspired ice cream sandwiches may have begun as a rebellion to our budding occupations—Natasha as an architect-in-training and Freya as a project manager for affordable housing development—but they became delicious platforms to show off our expertise.

Making a business out of ice cream sandwiches brought fun, whimsy, and adventure into our lives at a time when we both could have followed conventional paths. We were young, we were inspired, and what did we have to lose, besides our savings, homes, and dignity?

Though Freya's Ivy League education at Cornell never prepared her for the trials and tribulations of the mobile food game, her business acumen told her that something about this wacky ice cream sandwich idea could work. For Natasha, becoming an ice cream sandwich entrepreneur was a great way to implement her UCLA School of Architecture master's thesis on "Farchitecture" without taking the traditional path as an architect.

WTF IS FARCHITECTURE?

Food + Architecture, or "Farchitecture," was born when a professor likened one of Natasha's building models to a layer cake. That was her lightbulb moment, since her next model was an actual layer cake. It occurred to her that the ultimate edible structure was an ice cream sandwich—a cookie roof and floor with ice cream walls. That would eventually inspire us to name our creations after some of our heroes. Anyone for a Richard Meyer Lemon sandwich (Vegan Ginger Molasses Cookie with Meyer Lemon Gelato)? How about a Frank Behry (Snickerdoodle Cookie with Strawberries & Cream Gelato)? Introducing architectural tidbits via ice cream sandwiches was a great way to get people talking about architecture in general. And what could be a more fun, delicious conduit to bring architecture, which is, after all, a public profession, to the people? Making ice cream sandwiches proved to be the ultimate way to build out our flavor blueprints.

The name Coolhaus is a triple entendre, a play on Bauhaus, the influential modernist design movement of the 1920s and 1930s; Rem Koolhaas, the famous Dutch architect and theorist who challenged the mantra "form follows function"; and the fact that an ice cream sandwich is, indeed, a "cool house."

REM KOOLHAAS, THE PATRON SAINT OF OUR ICE CREAM SANDWICHES

The Dutch architect Rem Koolhaas is our hero. And he's more than just an architect: He's a Cornell grad (like Freya). He's a Harvard professor. He's also a journalist, writer, and cofounder of *Volume Magazine*. He's a filmmaker. He's a winner of the world's highest architectural honor, the Pritzker Architecuture Prize. And, above all, he's provocative. Some of his major works include the Serpentine Gallery Pavilion in London, the Torre Bicentenario in Mexico City, the Seoul National University Museum of Art, the Seattle Central Library, and Maison à Bordeaux in France. It is Koolhaas's interdisciplinary approach to everything he does that inspired us to meld the world of ice cream with architecture. Each and every recipe in this book—and, in fact, the whole Coolhaus brand—is a tribute to him.

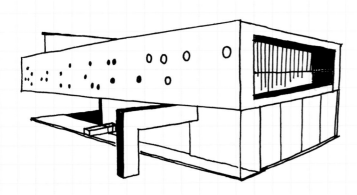

Maison à Bordeaux

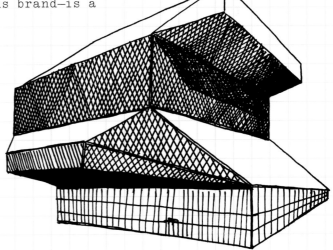

Seattle Central Library

Coolhaus (*Kool*-house), noun

1   An architecture-inspired ice cream sandwich. The Coolhaus ice cream sandwich consists of all-natural, homemade ice creams in classic and seasonal varieties, packed between two cookies of your choice.

2   An ice cream sandwich truck with chrome rims and a pink top (formerly a postal van). The Coolhaus truck is happily driven by architects, designers, developers, artists, bakers, actors, writers, musicians, and people from other walks of life.

3   A thinker. A thinker about reclaiming public and urban space for eating and gathering, when and where it is least expected. A Coolhaus thinks about how to reinvent or redesign food with an epicurean sensibility but also with an eye toward sustainability and minimal waste. A Coolhaus is passionate about food—where it comes from, how it is made, and how it is given to the eater. A Coolhaus has a curiosity for the day-to-day gastro-experience and a devotion to social merriment.

A mutual friend introduced us. She told us that we have the "same kind of brain." We instantly hit it off and, unsurprisingly, talked about food and architecture the whole time.

We started dating, and the business partnership came shortly after. Natasha was the big-picture idea person, creating flavors and not worrying too much about costs or production. Freya became the numbers and operations girl, putting her background in real estate development and finance to good use. We had the perfect complementary relationship that extended from the personal to the professional, and we had the same vision, which is what mattered most.

We began by making ice cream and cookies for friends. We didn't let the lack of a real production plant keep us from starting our dream business. We cooked anywhere we could, even after we set fire to Freya's mom's kitchen while preheating the oven. (How could we know there was a pizza sitting in there? Freya's mom has since lifted her kitchen ban.)

This unofficial but extremely serious hobby suddenly turned into a business. We hunted down recipes and developed our own tweaks. Before we knew it, we were planning our launch. We went on Craigslist and bought a dilapidated postal truck for $2,900 from three gangsta thugs who were, we suspect, using it to sell pot. They looked us up and down and asked, "What do you want this for?"

We chirpily told them, "We're going to sell all-natural, organic ice cream sandwiches!" They must have thought that was quaint, so they offered us a discount on some cases of Pepsi, which we politely declined.

15

We pulled off our first gig at the Coachella Valley Music and Arts Festival in Southern California in April 2009 with a mostly under-the-influence staff. Coachella is the Woodstock-meets-Lollapalooza of our generation, with a bunch of different performers from different genres playing. Back then, it was only one weekend but has since become so popular that it has been extended to two. There were a lot of great acts playing that year—The Killers, The Cure, M.I.A, Morrissey, the Yeah Yeah Yeahs. We didn't get to see any of them because we were working, but we could hear the rock/indie/hip-hop music wafting over from the stage, and it became our soundtrack. Today, it remains a huge part of our brand. "Coolhaus Radio," the playlist you'll hear at our shops and coming from our trucks, truly reflects a part of who we are.

Luck and persistence got us into Coachella. We offhandedly mentioned to a friend that we were thinking about selling our ice cream sandwiches at Coachella and that we had submitted an application but hadn't heard back. Our friend said he happened to know the CFO of Goldenvoice, the event's organizer, and he'd see what he could do. We obsessively followed up, and soon, someone contacted us, saying Coachella wanted to give us a shot selling in the campgrounds. (At that time there weren't any food trucks at Coachella—we were among the first.)

It was just four weeks before the festival when we got the go-ahead. We didn't have any production in place. We didn't have a factory. Our truck wasn't even up and running. But we were in, and there was no turning back.

The first thing we had to figure out was how to produce all those cookies and ice cream on our own at an event attended by a hundred thousand people. Then it dawned on us: This was not your average bake sale. We knew we couldn't possibly do it all, so we thought . . . how do other companies do this? Thanks to a handy Google search, we found out about "co-packers."

Co-packers are manufacturers that make your recipes, and you buy the finished goods back from them wholesale; the product belongs to you. This was completely foreign to us. We started Googling "ice cream co-packers" and "cookie co-packers" and came up with a local guy who seemed to have a substantial production company. (He does all the ice cream for Trader Joe's.) When we told him we needed five hundred gallons of ice cream for Coachella, he started laughing. His minimum was ten thousand gallons, but he agreed to help us anyway. It was our first introduction to the world of food production.

The next thing we had to do was figure out how to get our truck to the festival. It was completely broken down, and there was no way we could drive it 120 miles. While we were looking into insurance coverage, we discovered that an AAA Premier membership was only about $200 a year—and it came with two free 200-mile tows. That would be enough to get us to the desert and back.

We had to pretend that our little truck had broken down along the way so that AAA would tow it to Coachella, but when the tow truck arrived, we discovered that commercial vehicles aren't eligible. So we begged, saying, "We have this event! This is our dream! Please help us!"

The driver finally said, "Okay, okay. I'll do it

for you guys, but I'm letting you know that this is completely illegal and against company policy." Freya rode in the tow truck, and Natasha followed in another car. The truck was on a flatbed and barely made it underneath the overpasses—we took deep breaths each time and hoped that it would clear.

The atmosphere at Coachella was a free-for-all when we arrived. The pizza place next to us had grabbed all the electricity and power because it got there first. Since the campground is not as big a moneymaker as the concert grounds, we were at the bottom of the totem pole. And how would we be seen amid the sprawl of tents, many of which were like mini fortresses?

But the campground had its own good vibe. It was like a little community, with a karaoke lounge, a shower area, and a store. Everyone was really young: high school and college students, people in their twenties—hippy, hipster, drifter types. The campers had paid something like $60 for the whole weekend in this hot and dusty desert. The site, truth be told, was kind of gross. There were about fifteen thousand campers and only a hundred Porta Potties and probably an equal number of showers to share—by the end, no one was using either. The camper group was definitely grungier than the crowd inside, but they were a bunch of cheerful, cool young people just having a good time.

We realized some signage might help get us some attention. We didn't have a sign that said Coolhaus—just a banner reading **ICE CREAM SANDWICHES. ICED COFFEE. ICED TEA.** We did make Coolhaus tank tops out of American Apparel, and our staff wore those with cutoff jean shorts. The first night we didn't do very well at all. We definitely sold more drinks than ice cream sandwiches. The next day, we went to a FedEx Kinko's and made some signage. Before long, we had lots of signs but were still short on customers.

To draw attention to our truck, our friend Jeff strung Christmas lights all around. The other vendors had normal lighting, but our area was bright, like a beacon. We set out lawn chairs and tables so people could grab a sandwich or coffee and hang out.

The lights and atmosphere definitely got us some attention. We were selling the sandwiches for about $4, with four cookies and four ice creams to choose from. People were blown away by the sweet freedom. They could decide between our small selection of cookies—Chocolate Chip, Oatmeal Raisin, Snickerdoodle, and Double Chocolate—and our basic ice creams—Dirty Mint Chip, Vanilla, Lemon, and Strawberry. They could pick one of our creations, such as the Mint-imalism, make their own kooky cookie and ice cream combo (like Oatmeal Raisin Cookies and Dirty Mint Chip Ice Cream—weird!), or even have a different top and bottom cookie.

We were contracted to sell until 2:00 A.M. But there were always last-minute orders, and we wanted to make every dollar, so we didn't pack up and finish until 3:00 A.M. Then we'd have a "flash party" for thirty minutes, and by the time we'd go to bed, it was close to 4:00 A.M. Then we'd get up at 7:00 A.M. to serve coffee.

Managing the staff was a complete shitshow. We invited all our friends and told them that if they would work for free, they would get tickets to the festival for the entire weekend. We learned how hard it is to manage people, especially if they are your friends. Some of them had a little food service experience—others definitely did not. It was difficult to wrangle them. Sometimes they'd say, "I can't work right now, I want to go to the show!" And some of them roamed around trying to sell ice cream sandwiches while drunk and high. It was hard for us to expect anything more, since there was no clear "We are your bosses and this is our company" understanding. Luckily, Jeff and Sarah helped hold down the fort the whole time (and they've been to Coachella with us every year since).

Our friends Sean and Patrick, who are very good-looking actors, were great with the tent-to-tent sales. They'd take funny pictures with girls and toss the ice cream sandwiches to people, yelling, "Catch!" and people would throw dollar bills at them. They'd return with the money, and we'd just put it in the pile. There was no inventory tracking. There was no tracking of anything, really. As the weekend went on, we became more serious and started to pay attention to the money a little more. But on the whole, we didn't know anything about anything.

Despite our inexperience, we gained momentum, and the ice cream sandwiches started to sell pretty well. One of the most popular flavor combinations was basic chocolate chip cookies with vanilla ice cream. We called it "The Claaaassic." (Now it's known as the "Mies Vanilla Rohe," after the famous German architect.) To this day, it's the sandwich people order most.

It sunk in that we were on to something when we started to get groupies. One customer was a two-sandwiches-a-day kind of guy. He'd come by for his first at 7:00 A.M., and he'd pay $20 because he was such a big fan. Another guy had a little tattoo kit in his beret, and he kept coming up and offering to trade a tattoo for an ice cream sandwich. He would roll and unroll his kit, which looked like a weird heroin setup because of all the vials and needles. Another guy had eaten too many mushrooms and ran over in a panic saying that he needed something chewy. We scrambled to help by finding him the chewiest chocolate cookie we had.

But our biggest, and best, groupies from Coachella were Chris and Randy. One of them eventually became one of our first investors. Tall, white, lanky guys in their early twenties who sported hipster fanny packs and pants rolled up to their knees, they were Iraq war vets who had been in the air force and used their benefits to enroll in art school.

We left Coachella with some profit, some groupies, an investor, and a lot of energy and inspiration. Then the media frenzy started. While we were being towed home, *Curbed LA* posted about us. The post hit a nerve and went viral. Then we were on Apartment Therapy, Dwell, and *Los Angeles* magazine. Twitter alerts started lighting up our BlackBerries—about every five seconds! It was instant and insane, especially since at this point, the truck still didn't move. It didn't even have a door on it. But suddenly, our dream had become reality.

Our families and some friends were concerned—were we *really* going to ditch promising careers for ice cream sandwiches? We had a good feeling about it, though, and went with our instincts. From one dilapidated truck, we have now grown to fleets in Los Angeles, New York City, Dallas, and Austin; two California storefronts; an online shop; distribution in retailers across the country, including Whole Foods; and more.

Our employees and fans have drunk the Coolhaus Kool-Aid, and together, finally, we found ourselves responsible for a movement of cool-kid food. Sweet, fun, delicious—but in no way junk.

—NATASHA AND FREYA, 2014

BEFORE YOU BEGIN: TOOLS

Just as an architect needs a drafting board and a builder needs hammers and nails, cooks need their tools, too. Here's what you need to engineer the best Coolhaus sandwiches.

`TOOLS`

FOR ICE CREAM:

An ice cream maker. There are two general kinds: gel canister and compressor. (We don't recommend using the old-fashioned bucket ice cream makers—they are labor-intensive and messy.)

Gel canisters are otherwise known as "freezer bowl" models; basically you freeze the removable bowl before churning the base into a frozen state. They are gently priced, usually under $100. We recommend the Cuisinart ICE-21 gel canister ice cream maker for its ease of use, reasonable price, and consistent results. Ice cream made in a gel canister needs to be frozen for about 2 hours before serving, for a firm texture.

TIPS FOR USING GEL CANISTER ICE CREAM MAKERS:

- Clear out your freezer. The bowls can take up quite a bit of space.
- Plan ahead. The bowls usually need to be frozen overnight (check the manufacturer's instructions). The colder the bowl, the faster and better the ice cream freezes.
- Buy an extra freezer bowl. If you want to make more than one flavor at a time, one bowl will

always be completely frozen and ready to use.

- Do not take the bowl out of the freezer until ready for use. They can defrost very quickly.

Compressors have a built-in freezing mechanism. They are considered "professional quality" and are more expensive, from $200 to $1,000. They are convenient since you don't have to pre-freeze the bowl before use (freeing up your freezer space), and they produce an immediate firm consistency. We recommend the Simac and Cuisinart ICE-100 compressors for their ease of use and great results.

TIPS FOR USING COMPRESSOR ICE CREAM MAKERS:

- Let compressors run on the "chill" setting for at least 5 minutes to reach the proper temperature before making ice cream.

TIPS FOR USING ALL ICE CREAM MAKERS:

- Each brand has its own distinct operating instructions. Be sure to read the manufacturer's instructions carefully before use.

OTHER USEFUL TOOLS FOR ICE CREAM MAKING:

- Whisk
- Cooking thermometer
- 4-quart saucepan
- 4-quart pitcher (with lid) for storing and pouring the base
- 4-quart airtight containers for storing the ice cream

- Kitchen scale
- Liquid and dry measuring spoons and cups
- Microplane zester
- Immersion blender
- Blender or food processor
- Rubber spatula
- Large wooden mixing spoons
- Ice cream scoop
- Fine-mesh sieve
- Sifter

FOR COOKIES:
- Hand mixer or stand mixer
- Two baking sheets (half-sheet pans work best)
- Mixing bowls of various sizes
- Mixing spoon
- Rubber spatula
- Cooling rack
- Kitchen scale

FOR TOPPINGS:
- Candy thermometer

SOURCES

Some of the ingredients for our more exotic flavors may not be easy to find in your corner supermarket. Here are some recommended sites for general ingredients. (We also recommend sites for specialty ingredients within the recipes.)

www.penzeys.com
www.culinarydistrict.com
www.kalustyans.com

TIPS & TROUBLESHOOTING

Ice cream and cookies are pretty hard to ruin, and once you make one or two batches, the process becomes second nature. That said, we found ways to screw things up when we were first starting out. But we look at it this way: We made mistakes so that you don't have to! Here are some paths to pursue and pitfalls to avoid to achieve perfection.

- **Don't overcook the base.** Beware of curdling the base when cooking it. This happens when the base gets too hot too quickly. If it starts to have the consistency of scrambled eggs, it's overcooked. Scrambled egg ice cream is not in our preferred repertoire of flavors (unless bacon is involved).

- **Don't overchurn/overfreeze the ice cream.** When the ice cream comes out of the maker, it should have the consistency of soft serve. If it is like a stick of butter, it is overchurned and will be rock-hard after freezing. The thermometer reading should be 20 degrees for a properly frozen ice cream. *To fix overfrozen ice cream:* Melt down the ice cream with 30-second zaps in the microwave until it is liquid; strain out the mix-ins; mix with an immersion blender or hand mixer; add the mix-ins; then refreeze. Do not do this more than once, as you will be asking for a bacteria fest in your ice cream. If your ice cream is overfrozen again, throw it away and start over.

- **Add alcohol at the end of the process.** Alcohol has a high freezing point, but adding spirits at the end doesn't impede the freezing process.

- **Use sorbet strategies.** If the sorbet comes out too slushy, add more water a tablespoon at a time as you continue to churn it in the ice cream maker until it reaches the desired consistency. If the sorbet seems too hard, add more sugar. For more sorbet tips, see page 165.

- **Know your oven's true temperature.** Ovens can vary wildly in the reliability of their thermostats. Use an oven thermometer to double-check yours. And always check cookies at their minimum baking time for doneness to avoid overbaking. For more cookie tips, see page 184.

FOR BEST RESULTS

- **Make it fresh and keep it cold.** Get the base into the fridge to chill as quickly as possible to prevent spoilage, and do not store it for longer than 5 days.

- **Flavor comes first.** Use the freshest, best ingredients you can find for best results.

- **Plan ahead.** Making the ice creams in this book is a 2-day process, because you'll need to refrigerate the base at least overnight (unless you use our eggless or sorbet base). And if you are using a gel canister machine, always make sure your bowls have been in the freezer for 12 to 24 hours.

- **Make space.** Don't forget to make room for your base in the fridge and room for the final product in the freezer.

- **Bump up the flavor.** Cold mutes the flavor of ingredients, so use your taste buds and don't be afraid to err on the side of generosity when adding spices, herbs, mix-ins, and other flavorings.

- **Mix-ins come last.** As a rule of thumb, save the mix-ins until the end of the freezing process for even distribution and to prevent them from sinking to the bottom.

- **Make it ahead.** Freeze ice cream for at least 2 hours before serving, for the best consistency. Our ice creams have a soft-serve consistency when the machine finishes the process. Further freezing in an airtight storage container is necessary for firmness.

- **Never store ice cream, gelato, or sorbet in the canister.** Do not store ice cream in the canister, since it may stick to the sides of the container and damage the bowl.

- **Watch the shelf life.** Since our ice creams, gelatos, and sorbets are all-natural, with no preservatives, they should not be kept for longer than 2 weeks. Refrigerated cookie dough should be used within 2 weeks. Frozen cookie dough can be kept for up to 3 months.

SWIRLING TIPS FOR ICE CREAM

An artful swirl in an ice cream not only is functional, providing an even distribution of the swirled ingredient, but makes the ice cream look pretty. Keep these tips in mind for recipes that call for a swirl:

- Put a little bit of the swirl ingredient in a large, cold bowl, add all the ice cream as quickly as possible, then drizzle the remaining swirl ingredient on top. Draw a rubber spatula through the ice cream 3 to 4 times.

- Use an economy of motion when swirling: A few broad circular gestures with a rubber spatula usually does the trick.

- A little bit of a swirl ingredient goes a long way; be careful not to overdo it or the inclusions will permeate the base too much.
- When you're finished swirling, place the bowl in the freezer and allow the ice cream to firm up for 20 to 30 minutes before transferring it to an airtight storage container.

BUILDING THE PERFECT SANDWICH

- **Make the sandwich.** Place 1 cookie top side down on a work surface. Scoop 1 to 2 scoops (we use a 4-ounce scoop) of hard ice cream, gelato, or sorbet on top. Place another cookie top side up on top of the ice cream and press down lightly to even the filling and stick the sandwich together.
- **Freeze the entire sandwich.** Freezing the sandwich as a whole unit makes it easier to eat, with less melty ice cream spilling out the sides. Homemade Coolhaus ice cream sandwiches are good to go after a minimum of 1½ hours in the freezer and will keep for up to 2 weeks.
- **Most important: Have fun!** There shouldn't be anything dull about making ice cream and cookies. Invite friends, have a party, and feel free to experiment! Believe us, there's nothing more satisfying than building your own Coolhaus dream sandwich.

ICE CREAMS, GELATOS & SORBETS: WHAT'S THE DIFFERENCE?

Ice cream is a frozen dairy dessert that combines water, butterfat, sugar, and flavoring. Ours are custard-based and made with milk, cream, eggs, sugar, and inclusions. These elements are churned together, which whips air into the base. We strive for a lusciously creamy texture with a strong layering of flavor.

Gelato is the Italian word for ice cream, though there are some distinct differences. Gelato is usually denser and stickier in texture, with less air and less butterfat. Our gelato base includes milk, sugar, and eggs, but no cream.

Sorbet contains no dairy and has an icy, more granular texture than ice cream and gelato. It's made from frozen water, sugar, and flavorings.

Got it? Good. Our recipes are very easy for home chefs of all calibers—beginner to pro. With each one, we include a "skyscraper" rating system.

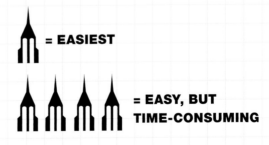

= EASIEST

= EASY, BUT TIME-CONSUMING

YOU'RE READY TO START!

ICE CREAM FOUNDATIONS

If you master these bases (foundations), you are guaranteed success with every recipe in this book. We use a simple French custard base (essentially a crème anglaise) for our ice creams with a lot of egg yolks for our signature rich, smooth texture. The eggs are a natural stabilizer, so the ice cream doesn't overfreeze, and you don't have to use the artificial gums and stabilizers found in most store-bought products. If you have an egg allergy, don't have time for the 2-day process, or simply prefer less richness to your ice cream, our recipes also come out fine with our quick-and-easy eggless base.

2 cups whole milk

2 cups heavy cream

1¼ cups granulated sugar

8 large egg yolks

PLAIN CUSTARD BASE

MAKES ABOUT: 1½ quarts | **ACTIVE TIME:** 10 to 15 minutes

Use the freshest eggs available for best results. If possible, refrigerate the base for a full 24 hours—the longer, the better. We like to chill our bases in plastic or stainless-steel pitchers with airtight lids for easy pouring into the ice cream maker after chilling.

1 In a 4-quart saucepan, combine milk, cream, and half of sugar. Set over high heat, and cook, stirring occasionally, until mixture comes to a boil, about 5 minutes.

2 Meanwhile, in a medium bowl, whisk yolks and remaining sugar until smooth, heavy, and pale yellow, about 30 seconds.

3 When cream mixture just comes to a boil, whisk, remove from heat, and, in a slow stream, pour half of cream mixture over yolk-sugar mixture, whisking constantly until blended.

4 Return pan to stovetop over low heat. Whisking constantly, stream yolk-cream mixture back into pan.

5 With a wooden spoon, continue stirring until mixture registers 165 to 180 degrees on an instant-read thermometer, about 2 minutes. Do not heat above 180 degrees, or eggs in base will scramble. Mixture should be slightly thickened and coat back of spoon, with steam rising, but not boiling. (If you blow on the back of the spoon and the mixture ripples, you've got the right consistency.)

6 Pour base into a clean airtight container and refrigerate for 12 to 24 hours before using.

7 Use base within 3 to 5 days.

CHOCOLATE CUSTARD BASE

MAKES ABOUT: 1½ quarts | **ACTIVE TIME:** 10 to 15 minutes

Use the freshest eggs available for best results. If possible, refrigerate the base for a full 24 hours—the longer it's chilled, the better it is. We like to chill our bases in plastic or stainless-steel pitchers with airtight lids for easy pouring into the ice cream maker after chilling.

1 In a 4-quart saucepan, combine milk, cream, and half of sugar. Set over high heat, and cook, stirring occasionally, until mixture comes to a boil, about 5 minutes.

2 Meanwhile, in a medium bowl, whisk yolks and remaining sugar until smooth, heavy, and pale yellow, about 30 seconds.

3 When cream mixture just comes to a boil, whisk, remove from heat, and, in a slow stream, pour half of cream mixture over yolk-sugar mixture, whisking constantly until blended.

4 Return pan to stovetop over low heat. Whisking constantly, stream yolk-cream mixture back into pan.

5 With a wooden spoon, continue stirring until mixture registers 165 to 180 degrees on an instant-read thermometer, about 2 minutes. Do not heat above 180 degrees, or eggs in base will scramble. Mixture should be slightly thickened and coat back of spoon, with steam rising, but not boiling. (If you blow on the back of the spoon and the mixture ripples, you've got the right consistency.)

6 Remove from heat and immediately add chopped chocolate, whisking until smooth.

7 Pour base into a clean airtight container and refrigerate for 12 to 24 hours before using .

8 Use base within 3 to 5 days.

2 cups whole milk

2 cups heavy cream

1¼ cups granulated sugar

8 large egg yolks

¾ cup bittersweet chocolate (64% to 72% cacao), chopped (we recommend Scharffen Berger, Valrhona, Trader Joe's, TCHO, or Mast Brothers)

TIP:

To make a basic chocolate ice cream, process base in an ice cream maker according to manufacturer's instructions. Transfer to an airtight storage container and freeze for a minimum of 2 hours.

3 cups heavy cream

2 cups half-and-half

1¾ cups granulated sugar

1 teaspoon natural vanilla extract

EGGLESS BASE

MAKES ABOUT: 2 quarts | **ACTIVE TIME:** 2 to 3 minutes

This quick-and-easy base is often referred to as "Philly-style," because of the City of Brotherly Love's partiality to it. It's not only good for our ovoid-averse friends, but it can be made for ice cream "on demand," because it does not have to be refrigerated overnight as the custard base does. It's ready for ice cream making as soon as the sugar dissolves and the flavoring is added.

1 In a 4-quart saucepan, combine cream, half-and-half, sugar, and vanilla. Cook over low heat, stirring, until sugar is just dissolved, about 2 minutes.

2 Use immediately or refrigerate in a clean airtight container for 3 to 5 days.

ICE CREAMS & SANDWICHES

NOTE: "Active times" do not include the making of the bases.

CLASSIC

ROOT BEER FLOAT ICE CREAM

MAKES ABOUT: 1½ quarts | **ACTIVE TIME:** 1 hour 20 minutes to 1 hour 25 minutes

This ice cream smacks of sassafras, once the main ingredient in root beer soda until the FDA banned it for commercial use some forty years ago. (Something about liver damage and cancer.) That's enough for us not to use it, but if you've ever tasted sassafras tea, you'll recognize the earthy, maple-like, slightly spicy tinge in this flavor. You can almost taste the frothy root beer head.

1 Reserve ½ cup of root beer. Pour remaining root beer into a 4-quart saucepan and bring to a boil over high heat. Reduce heat to low and cook, stirring occasionally, until most of the water evaporates and root beer has reduced to about ½ cup, about 1 hour. Be careful not to overheat or it will turn to candy. Cool at room temperature.

2 Stir reduced root beer and reserved ½ cup root beer into base and mix well.

3 Process in an ice cream maker according to manufacturer's instructions.

4 Scrape into an airtight storage container. Freeze for a minimum of 2 hours before serving.

SUGGESTED COOKIE:

S'mores (page 209)

1 (2-liter) bottle root beer (we like Virgil's)

Plain Custard Base (page 28) or Eggless Base (page 30)

ALTERNATE PREPARATION:

Instead of making root beer syrup, buy root beer flavoring from a well-stocked baking shop or online (at a site such as Lorannoils .com). Add 1 teaspoon at a time, tasting after each addition, until you reach the desired flavor.

SUGGESTED COOKIES:

Double Chocolate (page 188) or Snickerdoodle (page 194)

COOLHAUS SANDWICH CREATIONS:

Peter Cook-ies and Cream: Snickerdoodle Cookies + Cookies & Sweet Cream Ice Cream (see Building the Perfect Sandwich, page 25)

Plain Custard Base (page 28) or Eggless Base (page 30)

6 to 8 Oreo sandwich cookies, chopped or smashed to desired size with a rolling pin

TIP:

Oreo cookies also make a great addition to the Chocolate Custard Base (page 29) or in Dirty Mint Chip Ice Cream (page 40), in place of the chocolate chips.

COOKIES & SWEET CREAM ICE CREAM

MAKES ABOUT: 1½ quarts | **ACTIVE TIME:** 15 to 20 minutes

Chocolate Oreo cookies give crunch, and the filling provides a nice sugary jolt to the cream base. Think of the joy you experience upon dipping an Oreo into a glass of milk. When sandwiched between Snickerdoodle Cookies, this is the most popular ice cream selection when we cater birthday parties for kids.

1 Process base in an ice cream maker according to manufacturer's instructions.

2 Transfer to a bowl and fold in cookie pieces.

3 Scrape into an airtight storage container. Freeze for a minimum of 2 hours before serving.

WHO IS
PETER COOK?

A knighted English architect, Sir Peter Cook was a cofounder of Archigram, an experimental design collective that was active during the 1960s and 1970s and has been called "the Beatles of architecture." He is currently the director of the Institute of Contemporary Arts in London and is a widely published author.

STYLE: Blobitecture (a movement of amoeba-shaped buildings)

MAJOR WORKS: Kunsthaus Graz, Graz, Austria; Olympic Stadium, London

WHY WE LOVE HIM: He's pushing eighty and keeps a blog. In the blog bio, Cook says he has a "love affair with the slithering, the swarming, and the spooky." Plus, he gamely ate his eponymous ice cream sandwich when we had a truck at the Southern California Institute of Architecture.

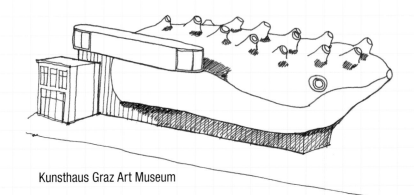

Kunsthaus Graz Art Museum

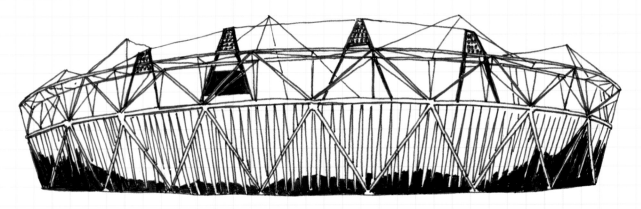

Olympic Stadium

Dirty Mint Chip Ice Cream (page 40)

SUGGESTED COOKIES:

Chocolate Chip (page 187) or Double Chocolate (page 188)

COOLHAUS SANDWICH CREATIONS:

The Buck-mint-ster Fuller: Chocolate Chip Cookies + Dirty Mint Chip Ice Cream (see Building the Perfect Sandwich, page 25)
Mint-imalism: Double Chocolate Cookies + Dirty Mint Chip Ice Cream

---

⅓ cup finely chopped fresh mint leaves

½ tablespoon dark brown sugar

¼ teaspoon kosher salt

Plain Custard Base (page 28) or Eggless Base (page 30), made with light brown sugar instead of granulated

½ cup mini semisweet chocolate chips (we like Guittard or Ghirardelli)

DIRTY MINT CHIP ICE CREAM

MAKES ABOUT: 1½ quarts | **ACTIVE TIME:** 20 to 30 minutes

We have news for you. That supermarket mint chip ice cream with the nuclear-green color? It doesn't have any mint leaves in it. It has mint oil or fake mint flavoring, and that nasty color comes from artificial coloring.

Real, fresh mint leaves give our Dirty Mint a fresh, cool intensity. Why is it "dirty"? Because we use brown sugar in the base, which gives the ice cream a deep caramel punch and a natural light brown color. It is also "dirty" because we don't strain out the mint. Leaving it in deepens the flavor the longer the ice cream is in the freezer.

(Warning: This has been known to convert mint ice cream haters.)

1 Stir mint leaves, dark brown sugar, and salt into base. Mix well.

2 Process in an ice cream maker according to manufacturer's instructions.

3 Transfer to a bowl and fold in chocolate chips.

4 Scrape into an airtight storage container. Freeze for a minimum of 2 hours before serving.

WHO IS
BUCKMINSTER FULLER?

R. Buckminster Fuller, a.k.a. "Bucky," was a certifiable American genius. And we say "certifiable" because he was actually the *president* of Mensa for nine years between 1974 and 1983, the year he died. Originally from Milton, Massachusetts, Fuller attended Milton Academy and later Harvard University, from which he was twice expelled (once for apparently using tuition money to throw a party for dancing girls in New York City—awesome!). The dude was so prolific that he held twenty-eight patents (he was also an inventor), wrote twenty-eight books, and received forty-seven honorary degrees. He was an architect, a poet, an environmentalist, and a humanitarian to boot.

STYLE: Futurist

MAJOR WORKS: Geodesic Dome; Dymaxion Car

WHY WE LOVE HIM: He was the grandnephew of Margaret Fuller, the famous nineteenth-century transcendentalist. He was also a global and sustainable thinker, well before his time. And he inspired the Spaceship Earth dome at Disney World's Epcot Center.

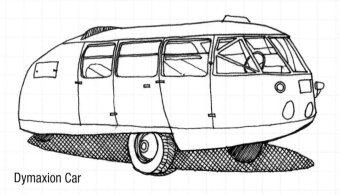

Dymaxion Car

Geodesic Dome

SUGGESTED COOKIE:

Chocolate Chip (page 187)

COOLHAUS SANDWICH CREATION:

Mies Vanilla der Rohe: Chocolate Chip Cookies + Tahitian Vanilla Bean Ice Cream (see Building the Perfect Sandwich, page 25)

1 Tahitian vanilla bean pod, split

Plain Custard Base (page 28), prepared up to final step of heating, or Eggless Base (page 30)

TAHITIAN VANILLA BEAN ICE CREAM

MAKES ABOUT: 1½ quarts **|** **ACTIVE TIME:** 15 to 20 minutes

Tahitian vanilla beans are expensive but worth every bit of the price. Their floral—almost chocolaty—flavor permeates the base for a scrumptious, aromatic result.

1 Scrape vanilla seeds from pod and stir into base (reserve pod). If using Plain Custard Base, continue with recipe, heating base to 165 to 180 degrees. Add reserved vanilla bean halves to base, pour base into a clean airtight container, and refrigerate for 12 to 24 hours.

2 Remove vanilla bean halves before processing. Process in an ice cream maker according to manufacturer's instructions.

3 Scrape into an airtight storage container. Freeze for a minimum of 2 hours before serving.

Tahitian Vanilla Bean Ice
Cream with Fried Chicken
Caramel (page 229)

WHO IS
MIES VAN DER ROHE?

German-born Ludwig Mies van der Rohe served as the last director of Bauhaus, the influential German school of modernist design, art, and architecture. A fan of steel and plate glass and a pioneer of the modernist movement, van der Rohe headed the Illinois Institute of Technology (then the Armour Institute) and made a lasting impression on the landscape of cultural, educational, and corporate structures.

STYLE: Less-Is-More Modernist

MAJOR WORKS: Seagram Building, New York City; Farnsworth House, Plano, Illinois; Neue Nationalgalerie, Berlin; Barcelona Pavilion, Barcelona

WHY WE LOVE HIM: His geometric simplicity is surprisingly poetic. Just as our Tahitian Vanilla Bean Ice Cream is far from plain vanilla, his style is graceful and subtly complex, highlighting the virtues of minimalist pleasure.

Seagram Building

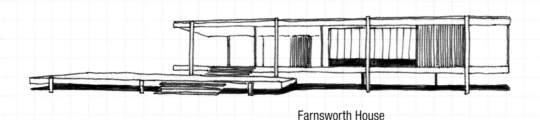

Farnsworth House

FRUITY

HEADS UP: Overripe fruit is perfect for fruity ice creams. The riper the fruit, the more sugar and the more pronounced the flavor. Plus, riper fruit is softer and easier to puree.

AÇAI BLUEBERRY WITH GOJI BERRIES ICE CREAM

MAKES ABOUT: 1½ quarts | **ACTIVE TIME:** 40 to 45 minutes

Putting açai and goji berries—healthy "superfruits"— in ice cream is a clever way of having your antioxidants and enjoying them, too. The chewy, cranberry-like dried goji berries add a slight crunch when frozen, while açai juice contributes a jammy tang. The blueberries balance the tartness.

Açai juice and dried goji berries can be found at Whole Foods and natural and health food markets.

1 In a heavy saucepan, combine blueberries, sugar, açai juice, and lemon juice and cook over low heat, stirring occasionally, until berries burst and mix thickens slightly, 15 to 20 minutes.

2 Strain mixture through a fine-mesh sieve into a bowl to remove seeds. Discard solids left in sieve. Set syrup aside to cool.

3 Process base in an ice cream maker according to manufacturer's instructions. Transfer to a bowl and fold in blueberry syrup to make an attractive swirl (see tips, page 24). Fold in goji berries.

4 Scrape into an airtight storage container. Freeze for a minimum of 2 hours before serving.

SUGGESTED COOKIES:

Double Chocolate (page 188) or Snickerdoodle (page 194)

½ cup fresh or frozen blueberries (Earthbound Farm and Safeway Organic are good frozen brands)

½ cup granulated sugar

½ cup açai juice

Juice of ½ lemon (about 2 tablespoons)

Plain Custard Base (page 28) or Eggless Base (page 30)

6 tablespoons dried goji berries

SUGGESTED COOKIE:

Oatmeal Raisin (page 191)

COOLHAUS SANDWICH CREATION:

Renzo Apple Pie-ano: Oatmeal Raisin Cookies + Baked Apple Ice Cream (see Building the Perfect Sandwich, page 25)

1 cup plain (not cinnamon) gourmet-brand applesauce (such as Whole Foods 365 Everyday Value or Trader Joe's Organic)

1½ teaspoons ground cinnamon

2 tablespoons light brown sugar

Pinch ground nutmeg

Pinch ground cloves

Pinch kosher salt

1 teaspoon natural vanilla extract

Plain Custard Base (page 28) or Eggless Base (page 30)

BAKED APPLE ICE CREAM

MAKES ABOUT: 1½ quarts | **ACTIVE TIME:** 20 to 25 minutes

Think fall apple-picking season in New England, with the nostalgic fragrances of cinnamon and clove wafting from the kitchen of a quaint country inn. In this reinvention of an aromatic classic, the mellowness of the fruit lingers well after the last lick.

1 Stir applesauce, cinnamon, brown sugar, nutmeg, cloves, salt, and vanilla into base and mix well with an immersion blender or a whisk.

2 Process in an ice cream maker according to manufacturer's instructions.

3 Scrape into an airtight storage container. Freeze for a minimum of 2 hours before serving.

WHO IS
RENZO PIANO?

Born into a family of builders in Italy, Renzo Piano had a predisposition for construction. His Shard building in London is the tallest skyscraper in Europe. He also recently designed the Art Institute of Chicago's new Modern Wing and is at work on the new Whitney Museum of American Art, which is between the High Line (see page 54) and the Hudson River in New York City. Piano's daughter, Lia Arduino, is also pursuing a career in architecture.

STYLE: High tech

MAJOR WORKS: Centre Georges Pompidou (with Gianfranco Franchini and Richard Rogers), Paris; Parco della Musica, Rome; New York Times Building, New York City

WHY WE LOVE HIM: Piano is a big believer in teamwork, judging from his collaborations with other established architects, such as Richard Rogers and Peter Rice. Plus, he's so cool that he even designed a Swatch watch, called the "Jelly Piano," which gives a nod to his Pompidou Centre design.

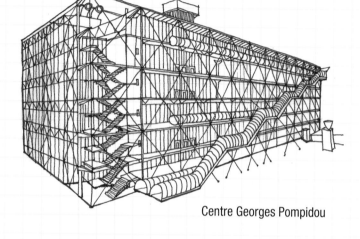

Centre Georges Pompidou

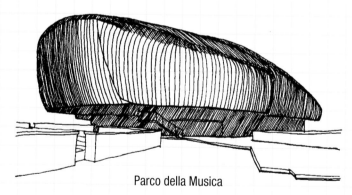

Parco della Musica

SUGGESTED COOKIE:

Snickerdoodle (page 194)

6 cups Froot Loops cereal, plus 2 tablespoons for garnish

Plain Custard Base (page 28), prepared up to refrigerating step, or Eggless Base (page 30)

FROOT LOOPS & MILK ICE CREAM

MAKES ABOUT: 1½ quarts | **ACTIVE TIME:** 20 to 25 minutes

We thought, wouldn't it be cool to make an ice cream in homage to one of our favorite cereals? This delicious ice cream brings back childhood guilty-pleasure memories of drinking the colorful milk at the bottom of our breakfast bowls. The hints of strawberry and orange are reminiscent of that rainbow milk, with the same sugary crunch.

The amount of cereal may seem like too much, but it nearly dissolves in the milk.

1 Put Froot Loops in a bowl and pour hot base over them. Let stand to get soggy. Using an immersion blender or a whisk, mix until smooth. If using Plain Custard Base, refrigerate as directed.

2 Process in an ice cream maker according to manufacturer's instructions.

3 Scrape into an airtight storage container. Freeze for a minimum of 2 hours before serving. Sprinkle remaining 2 tablespoons Froot Loops over ice cream for garnish.

KEY LIME PIE ICE CREAM

MAKES ABOUT: 1½ quarts | **ACTIVE TIME:** 20 to 30 minutes

Our Key lime pie is so authentic because of its pale yellow (not artificial green) color and bright, tropically tangy taste. A natural candidate for an ice cream flavor, real Key lime pie filling is a custard made from egg yolks, much like our base. The perfect slice of Key lime pie is topped with fresh whipped cream to cut through the tartness—exactly what the creamy infusion in our ice cream does. Graham cracker pieces lend a pie crust texture: not too crunchy, with a wonderful, buttery edge.

1 Stir lime zest and lime juice into base. Mix well.

2 Process in an ice cream maker according to manufacturer's instructions.

3 Transfer to a bowl and fold in graham cracker pieces.

4 Scrape into an airtight storage container. Freeze for a minimum of 2 hours before serving.

SUGGESTED COOKIE:

Snickerdoodle (page 194)

COOLHAUS SANDWICH CREATION:

Highlime Pie: Snickerdoodle Cookies + Key Lime Pie Ice Cream (see Building the Perfect Sandwich, page 25)

Zest of 1 Key lime, grated on a Microplane

½ cup fresh Key lime juice (from 16 to 20 Key limes)

Plain Custard Base (page 28) or Eggless Base (page 30)

½ cup broken graham cracker pieces

WHAT IS
THE HIGH LINE?

A park built on an abandoned elevated train line, the High Line in New York City is a genius example of urban reuse. Unveiled in 2011, it runs from the Meatpacking District in Lower Manhattan up to 30th Street in Chelsea. Designed by James Corner Field Operations and Diller Scofidio + Renfro, the greenway is a favorite retreat for strolling New Yorkers. Our truck was a fixture at the High Line when it debuted; our Highlime Pie Ice Cream sandwich was a popular order.

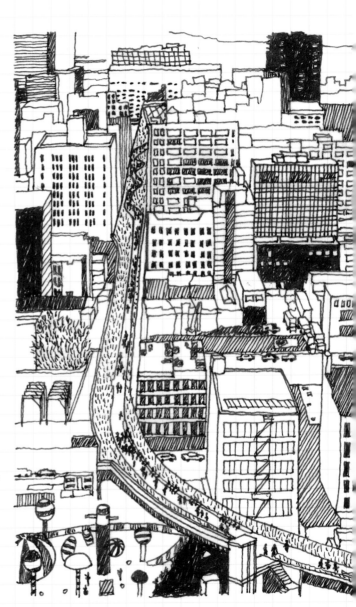

Long View

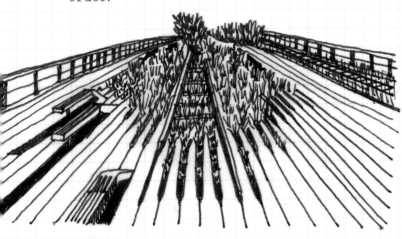

Close-Up

SANTIGOLD STRAWBERRY ICE CREAM

MAKES ABOUT: 1½ quarts | **ACTIVE TIME:** 20 to 25 minutes

SUGGESTED COOKIE:

Snickerdoodle (page 194)

We made artist-inspired flavors for Coachella, and the singer Santigold chose strawberry. We couldn't resist adding gold sprinkles to her favorite flavor as a tribute to her golden-throated sound.

Our strawberry is a simple, vivid palate awakener that sings in the mouth—the kind of feeling that makes you want to "singjay" (Santigold's deejay-like vocal style), as she does in her song "Creator." Flecks of gold create the impression of a gemstone: A scoop looks like a beautiful rose quartz with a shimmer of fool's gold. We recommend putting on her music while crafting this flavor and rocking out in the downtime!

1 cup strawberry puree (fresh or made from defrosted frozen organic strawberries), strained through a fine-mesh sieve to remove seeds (Earthbound Farm and Safeway Organic are good frozen brands)

Plain Custard Base (page 28) or Eggless Base (page 30)

½ cup gold sprinkles (see Tip)

1 Stir strawberry puree into base. Mix well with an immersion blender or a whisk.

2 Process in an ice cream maker according to manufacturer's instructions.

3 Transfer to a bowl and fold in gold sprinkles.

4 Scrape into an airtight container. Freeze for a minimum of 2 hours before serving.

TIP:

Gold sprinkles can be found at specialty baking supply stores (see Sources, page 23).

SUGGESTED COOKIE:

Oatmeal Raisin (page 191)

FOR BASE

2 cups whole milk

8 large egg yolks

1 cup heavy cream

1¼ cups granulated sugar

2 cups full-fat plain Greek yogurt (such as Fage or Chobani; see headnote)

¾ cup hulled and sliced fresh or frozen strawberries (Earthbound Farm and Safeway Organic are good frozen brands)

¾ cup fresh or frozen raspberries

¾ cup fresh or frozen blueberries

1 cup granulated sugar

YOGURT & BERRIES ICE CREAM

MAKES ABOUT: 1½ quarts | **ACTIVE TIME:** 20 to 30 minutes

The custard base for this ice cream is made with Greek yogurt and uses less cream than our customary base. Strawberries, raspberries, and blueberries sweeten up the tartness of the yogurt.

Use only full-fat yogurt to make this ice cream—preferably the most dense, thick, decadent one you can find.

1. **Make base:** In a 4-quart saucepan, combine milk, cream, and half of sugar. Set over high heat, and cook, stirring occasionally, until mixture comes to a boil, about 5 minutes.

2. Meanwhile, in a medium bowl, whisk yolks and remaining sugar until smooth, heavy, and pale yellow, about 30 seconds.

3. When cream mixture just comes to a boil, whisk, remove from heat, and, in a slow stream, pour half of cream mixture over yolk-sugar mixture, whisking constantly until blended.

4. Return pan to stovetop over low heat. Whisking constantly, stream yolk-cream mixture back into pan.

5. With a wooden spoon, continue stirring until mixture registers 165 to 180 degrees on an instant-read thermometer, about 2 minutes. Do not heat above 180 degrees, or eggs in base will scramble. Mixture should be slightly thickened and coat back of spoon, with steam rising, but not boiling. (If you blow on the back of the spoon and the mixture ripples, you've got the right consistency.)

6. Add yogurt to base and mix well.

7. Pour into a clean airtight container and refrigerate for 12 to 24 hours.

8 Process in an ice cream maker according to manufacturer's instructions.

9 Meanwhile, in a blender, puree berries with sugar. Strain through a fine-mesh sieve into a bowl to remove seeds. Discard seeds left in sieve.

10 Transfer churned ice cream to a bowl and fold in berry puree to make an attractive swirl (see tips, page 24).

11 Scrape into an airtight storage container. Freeze for a minimum of 2 hours before serving.

SUGGESTED COOKIES:

Double Chocolate (page 188) or
Snickerdoodle (page 194)

1 serrano chile, stemmed and
seeded

½ cup pineapple puree (from 1 cup
pineapple chunks)

Plain Custard Base (page 28) or
Eggless Base (page 30)

1 tablespoon finely chopped fresh
cilantro leaves

SPICY PINEAPPLE-CILANTRO-CHILE ICE CREAM

MAKES ABOUT: 1½ quarts | **ACTIVE TIME:** 25 to 30 minutes

The sharp bite of serrano chile cuts through the sugary pineapple, with cilantro unifying the opposites. It's a surprising blend, with a piquant piña colada-like flavor—the sort of ice cream you keep eating to taste all the elements as they unfold on your tongue.

1 Puree chile and pineapple in a bowl with an immersion blender (or in a regular blender or food processor) until well combined.

2 Mix pineapple-serrano puree into base with an immersion blender or a whisk.

3 Process in an ice cream maker according to manufacturer's instructions.

4 Transfer to a bowl and fold in cilantro.

5 Scrape into an airtight storage container. Freeze for a minimum of 2 hours before serving.

BOOZY

If you want to eliminate the alcohol from our boozy recipes yet keep the flavor of the liquor, use this method to boil off the alcohol before adding it to the recipe. The resulting liquid will be about half of what the recipe calls for, but do not add more—the flavor will be intensified.

1 Pour the alcohol into a wide saucepan with a lid.

2 Set the pan over medium heat and heat the alcohol until it just starts to bubble.

3 Take a long-handled lighter and ignite the alcohol in the pan. Keep the lid nearby to quickly smother the flame if it threatens to get out of control.

4 The flame should subside after about 1 minute. When it dies down, turn off the burner and drop the lid on the pan to be sure the fire is extinguished.

5 Let cool, and then add the alcohol to the base.

BANANAS FOSTER ICE CREAM

MAKES ABOUT: 1½ quarts | **ACTIVE TIME:** 20 to 30 minutes

This torched, caramelized banana flavor combines all the excitement of tableside presentation with the sweet, bracing edge of flambéed rum and finishes with smooth, buttery, salty, and sweet notes.

1 Mix pureed bananas into base with an immersion blender or a hand mixer.

2 Process in an ice cream maker according to manufacturer's instructions.

3 Meanwhile, in a wide saucepan, melt butter and brown sugar together and bring to a boil over medium heat. Add rum, let flame, bring back to a boil, and turn off heat. Let caramel cool.

4 Transfer churned ice cream to a bowl and fold in caramel to make an attractive swirl (see tips, page 24).

5 Scrape into an airtight storage container. Freeze for a minimum of 2 hours before serving.

SUGGESTED COOKIES:

Double Chocolate (page 188), Double Chocolate Sea Salt (page 190), or Maple Flapjack (page 200)

COOLHAUS SANDWICH CREATION:

Bananas Norman Foster: Double Chocolate Cookies + Bananas Foster Ice Cream (see Building the Perfect Sandwich, page 25)

---

3 ripe bananas, pureed

Plain Custard Base (page 28) or Eggless Base (page 30)

½ stick (4 tablespoons) butter

¼ cup packed light brown sugar

¼ cup dark rum (such as Appleton Estate)

WHO IS
NORMAN FOSTER?

That's "Sir" Norman Foster to you. Raised in blue-collar Manchester, England, Foster was knighted in 1990 and, in 1999, was made a life peer with the title of Baron Foster of Thames Bank, of Reddish in the County of Greater Manchester. In addition to collecting titles, Foster is also credited with pioneering green building and design practices.

STYLE: Imaginative modernism

MAJOR WORKS: The Gherkin (Swiss Re Tower, 30 St Mary Axe), London; Wembley Stadium, London; Valencia Congress Centre, Spain; Millennium Bridge, London

WHY WE LOVE HIM: His name is perfect for this flavor. Foster's Gherkin building in London sort of resembles a banana, and the ice cream's aristocratic deliciousness is certainly fit for a baron.

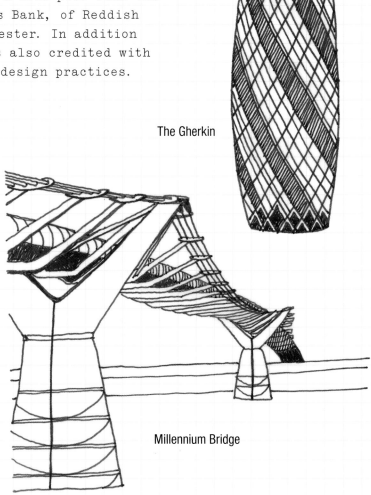

The Gherkin

Millennium Bridge

BANANA, HONEY & MEZCAL ICE CREAM

MAKES ABOUT: 1½ quarts | **ACTIVE TIME:** 20 to 25 minutes

This ripe, tropical, sticky, and smoky smack-in-the-face ice cream features three ingredients that go well together because they evoke the landscape of Central America. The centerpiece of that harmony is mezcal, a close sibling of tequila. Harvested from the agave plant, the spirit has an herbal-charcoal flavor that balances the sweetness of the honey and mingles nicely with the tender texture of the banana.

1 Stir honey into base. If using Plain Custard Base, proceed with recipe, heating and refrigerating as directed.

2 Mix bananas and salt into cooled base with an immersion blender or a whisk. Mix well.

3 Process in an ice cream maker according to manufacturer's instructions, adding mezcal during last 2 minutes of churning.

4 Scrape into an airtight storage container. Freeze for a minimum of 2 hours before serving.

SUGGESTED COOKIES:

Double Chocolate Sea Salt (page 190) or Gluten-Free Coconut Almond Chocolate Chip (page 214)

2 tablespoons honey

Plain Custard Base (page 28), prepared up to final heating step, or Eggless Base (page 30)

3 very ripe bananas

Pinch kosher salt

¼ cup mezcal añejo or reposado

TRY THIS:

Serve with a sprinkling of earthy-smoky worm salt (*sal de gusano*) for an authentic Mexican twist. Yes, it's made with real dried and ground worms. Find some online at www.firebox.com.

SUGGESTED COOKIE:

Double Chocolate Sea Salt (page 190)

1 cup Belgian abbey-style dark beer (such as Allagash Black Stout)

Plain Custard Base (page 28) or Eggless Base (page 30)

6 ounces hard pretzels, broken into ¼- to ½-inch pieces or to taste

BEER & PRETZEL ICE CREAM

MAKES ABOUT: 1½ quarts | **ACTIVE TIME:** 20 to 25 minutes

Salty, crunchy, malty, and caramel-y, this ice cream combines notes of toast and toffee, with a slight cocoa edge. It's a primal thrill, sort of like watching football. Serve it to the guys at a Super Bowl party.

1 Add beer to base. Mix well.

2 Process in an ice cream maker according to manufacturer's instructions.

3 Transfer to a bowl and fold in pretzel pieces.

4 Scrape into an airtight storage container. Freeze for a minimum of 2 hours before serving.

BLUEBERRY MOJITO ICE CREAM

MAKES ABOUT: 1½ quarts | **ACTIVE TIME:** 30 to 40 minutes

Sweet blueberries, caramel-y brown sugar. Bright lime, refreshing mint, and the smooth citrus of rum. These are the makings of the perfect beach ice cream. Eat near a palm tree and a roaring surf for best results.

1 In a heavy saucepan, combine blueberries, sugar, and lime juice. Cook over low heat, stirring, until berries burst and mixture thickens slightly and coats the back of a spoon, about 8 minutes.

2 Strain syrup through a fine-mesh sieve into a bowl to remove seeds. Discard solids left in sieve. Set syrup aside to cool.

3 Add mint and lime zest to base and stir well.

4 Process in an ice cream maker according to manufacturer's instructions. Add rum during last 2 minutes of churning.

5 Transfer churned ice cream to a bowl and fold in cooled blueberry syrup, making an attractive swirl (see tips, page 24).

6 Scrape into an airtight storage container. Freeze for a minimum of 2 hours before serving.

SUGGESTED COOKIES:

Double Chocolate Sea Salt (page 190) or Snickerdoodle (page 194)

½ cup fresh or frozen blueberries (Earthbound Farm and Safeway Organic are good frozen brands)

½ cup granulated sugar

Juice of ½ lime (about 2 tablespoons); grate zest first

2 tablespoons finely chopped fresh mint

Zest of 1 lime, grated on a Microplane

Plain Custard Base (page 28) or Eggless Base (page 30), made with 1¼ cups packed light brown sugar instead of granulated

¼ cup light rum

SUGGESTED COOKIES:

Red Velvet (page 204) or Double Chocolate Sea Salt (page 190)

½ cup chocolate stout (such as Rogue or Brooklyn Black)

Chocolate Custard Base (page 29)

6 ounces chocolate-covered pretzels, broken into ¼- to ½-inch pieces or to taste

CHOCOLATE STOUT & CHOCOLATE-COVERED PRETZELS

MAKES ABOUT: 1½ quarts | **ACTIVE TIME:** 20 to 25 minutes

This is what to serve when you have *girls* coming to your Super Bowl party. They dig the deep chocolate and malty, hoppy buzz of cacao and vanilla.

1 Add chocolate stout to base and mix well.

2 Process in an ice cream maker according to manufacturer's instructions.

3 Transfer to a bowl and fold in chocolate-covered pretzels.

4 Scrape into an airtight storage container. Freeze for a minimum of 2 hours before serving.

SUGGESTED COOKIES:

Pretzel Chocolate Chunk (page 202) or Snack Food Chocolate Chip (page 210)

½ stick (4 tablespoons) butter

8 (1-ounce) strips bacon

½ cup maple syrup

½ teaspoon sea salt

Plain Custard Base (page 28) or Eggless Base (page 30)

2 tablespoons bourbon

BOURBON BROWN BUTTER CANDIED BACON ICE CREAM

MAKES ABOUT: 1½ quarts | **ACTIVE TIME:** 40 to 45 minutes

This ice cream hits every point of the palate, with the salty, smoky bacon, the nutty, butterscotch tinge from the brown butter, the sweetness of molasses, and the warm punch of oaky bourbon.

1 In a small saucepan, melt butter over medium heat. Cook until it is a medium brown/caramel color, being careful not to burn it, about 4 minutes. Strain melted butter through a fine-mesh sieve into a small bowl. Set aside to cool.

2 In a large skillet, cook bacon strips over medium-low heat, turning, until just before crispy. Transfer to paper towels to drain and cool.

3 Finely dice cooled bacon. In a clean skillet, combine diced bacon and maple syrup and cook over medium-high heat for about 3 minutes, until syrup is thick and has reduced by half. Sprinkle with sea salt. Set candied bacon aside to cool.

4 Mix brown butter and candied bacon into base.

5 Process in an ice cream maker according to manufacturer's instructions. Add bourbon during last 2 minutes of churning.

6 Scrape into an airtight storage container. Freeze for a minimum of 2 hours before serving.

DIRTY MINT JULEP ICE CREAM

MAKES ABOUT: 1½ quarts | **ACTIVE TIME:** 20 to 30 minutes

SUGGESTED COOKIE:

Snickerdoodle (page 194)

We call this flavor "Landscape Bourbonism." The name was chosen by the James Corner Field Operations office when we launched the ice cream and treated the staff to it at a construction site in L.A.

Mint and Maker's Mark are a match made in heaven—the combination is sweet, refreshing, woodsy, and substantial. It's exactly like a mint julep, the traditional drink of the Kentucky Derby. It tastes even better if you wear a large hat and white gloves while you eat it.

⅓ cup finely chopped fresh mint leaves

½ tablespoon dark brown sugar

¼ teaspoon kosher salt

Plain Custard Base (page 28) or Eggless Base (page 30), made with packed light brown sugar instead of granulated

¼ cup bourbon, preferably Maker's Mark

1 Add mint leaves, dark brown sugar, and salt to base. Mix well.

2 Process in an ice cream maker according to manufacturer's instructions. Add bourbon during last 2 minutes of churning.

3 Scrape into an airtight storage container. Freeze for a minimum of 2 hours before serving.

WHAT IS

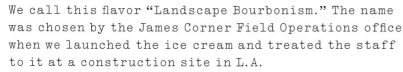

LANDSCAPE URBANISM?

Landscape Urbanism is the theory that landscape, not buildings, is the core to city planning. It stresses an organic use of infrastructure in urban areas. Architects at James Corner Field Operations, the firm of James Corner, embodied this theory in their design of New York City's High Line.

BOURBON MANHATTAN ICE CREAM

MAKES ABOUT: 1½ quarts | **ACTIVE TIME:** 15 to 20 minutes

This classic cocktail flavor is what happens when an ice cream social meets a sophisticated happy hour. The sexy smokiness of the bourbon fuses with a sweet zing from vermouth; syrupy Amarena dark cherries and bitters even it all out. The lingering finish brings up new notes of vanilla, oak, traces of cinnamon . . . the perfect scoop after a long day at the office.

1 Process base in an ice cream maker according to manufacturer's instructions. Add vermouth, bourbon, and bitters during last 2 minutes of churning.

2 Transfer to a bowl and fold in cherries.

3 Scrape into an airtight storage container. Freeze for a minimum of 2 hours before serving.

SUGGESTED COOKIE:

Double Chocolate Sea Salt (page 190)

Plain Custard Base (page 28) or Eggless Base (page 30)

2 tablespoons red vermouth (such as Cinzano or Martini)

¼ cup bourbon

Dash of Angostura bitters

12 Luxardo maraschino or Amarena cherries, quartered

TIP:

You can find Amarena cherries at gourmet stores or online at www.igourmet.com.

SUGGESTED COOKIES:

Oatmeal Raisin (page 191) or Maple Flapjack Cookie (page 200)

- 1 stick (8 tablespoons) butter
- ½ cup pecan pieces
- ½ teaspoon kosher salt
- ¾ cup dark corn syrup
- Plain Custard Base (page 28) or Eggless Base (page 30)
- ¼ cup bourbon, preferably Maker's Mark

BOURBON PECAN PIE ICE CREAM

MAKES ABOUT: 1½ quarts | **ACTIVE TIME:** 40 to 45 minutes

A visit to the Maker's Mark plant in Kentucky inspired this ice cream—the perfect Thanksgiving dessert for families who like to drink. Though any bourbon will get the job done, we highly recommend Maker's Mark for its distinctive flavor: toasty, with touches of mint, cocoa, and peanut butter. The creamy finish conjures pie, while pecans tossed in butter and dark corn syrup add a candy-coated crunch.

1   In a large skillet, melt butter over medium heat. Add pecan pieces and cook, stirring occasionally, until toasted, 5 to 10 minutes, removing pan from heat once butter starts to get foamy. Set aside to cool.

2   In a small saucepan, combine salt and corn syrup, and cook, stirring, over low to medium heat until mixture is candy-coated and sticky and registers about 235 degrees on a candy thermometer. Set aside to cool.

3   Process base in an ice cream maker according to manufacturer's instructions. Add bourbon during last 2 minutes of churning.

4   Transfer to a bowl and stir in pecan mixture.

5   Scrape into an airtight storage container. Freeze for a minimum of 2 hours before serving.

CHOCOLATE ORANGE COINTREAU ICE CREAM

MAKES ABOUT: 1½ quarts | **ACTIVE TIME:** 15 to 20 minutes

This is our homage to Terry's Chocolate Orange candy, the one that breaks apart into little chocolate pieces shaped like orange segments. The ice cream's straightforward chocolate-orange flavor is kicked up with the complex, spirited punch of Cointreau. We first served it at The Taste of LA at Paramount Studios—there was a two-hour line at the truck to try it. Customers said it was worth the wait!

1 **Prepare Chocolate Custard Base:** When cream mixture comes to a boil, stir in orange zest. Proceed with heating and refrigerating as directed.

2 Process in an ice cream maker according to manufacturer's instructions. Add Cointreau during last 2 minutes of churning.

3 Scrape into an airtight storage container. Freeze for a minimum of 2 hours before serving.

SUGGESTED COOKIE:

Gluten-Free Coconut Almond Chocolate Chip (page 214)

Chocolate Custard Base (page 29, prepared up to egg tempering step

Zest of 1 large orange, grated on a Microplane

¼ cup Cointreau

SUGGESTED COOKIE:

Double Chocolate Sea Salt (page 190)

¼ cup Guinness Extra Stout

1½ teaspoons instant coffee powder (such as Folgers)

¼ teaspoon kosher salt

¼ teaspoon natural vanilla extract

Plain Custard Base (page 28) or Eggless Base (page 30)

½ cup semisweet chocolate chips (we like Guittard or Ghirardelli)

GUINNESS CHOCOLATE CHIP ICE CREAM

MAKES ABOUT: 1½ quarts | **ACTIVE TIME:** 15 to 20 minutes

Imagine if you had an Irish coffee made with Guinness stout instead of whiskey. Coffee amps up the bitter chocolate profile of the creamy stout. This ice cream makes for a fantastic floater in a freshly drawn pint. Serve on St. Patrick's Day.

1 Add Guinness, coffee, salt, and vanilla to base. Mix well.

2 Process in an ice cream maker according to manufacturer's instructions.

3 Transfer to a bowl and fold in chocolate chips.

4 Scrape into an airtight storage container. Freeze for a minimum of 2 hours before serving.

HOT CHOCOLATE MEZCAL ICE CREAM

MAKES ABOUT: 1½ quarts | **ACTIVE TIME:** 15 to 20 minutes

We like to think of this flavor as a mistake that worked. When our friends at Scorpion Mezcal were on the East Coast in the deep winter, they made some hot chocolate samples spiked with mezcal. They put the container with the hot chocolate in the trunk and promptly forgot about it. When they opened the trunk later, it had frozen. They tasted it and called us immediately, suggesting that it become a Coolhaus flavor.

The afterburn of cayenne and cinnamon, plus the smolder of mezcal, adds heat to this ice cream. The final epiphany for us was pairing it with a Snickerdoodle cookie. The combo tastes just like a churro stick dipped in thick, gooey Mexican chocolate.

Make sure you use a Mexican (also called Ceylon) cinnamon stick, which is papery and soft, not hard.

1 Remove cinnamon stick before adding chocolate to base. Refrigerate as directed.

2 Add zest, cayenne pepper, and vanilla to base.

3 Process in an ice cream maker according to manufacturer's instructions. Add mezcal during last 2 minutes of churning.

4 Scrape into an airtight storage container. Freeze for a minimum of 2 hours before serving.

SUGGESTED COOKIE:

Snickerdoodle (page 194)

1 (3-inch) Mexican cinnamon stick (see headnote)

Chocolate Custard Base (page 29), made with cinnamon stick added to cream mixture before boiling

Zest of 1 orange, grated on a Microplane

½ teaspoon cayenne pepper

1 teaspoon natural vanilla extract

¼ cup mezcal añejo or reposado

TIP:

Find Mexican cinnamon sticks at www.mesamexicanfoods.com.

SUGGESTED COOKIES:

S'mores (page 209) or Oatmeal Raisin (page 191)

2 tablespoons butter, plus more for the pan

6 tablespoons packed light brown sugar

1 (8.5-ounce) can peaches, drained, juice reserved

1 cup pecan pieces

Pinch kosher salt

Plain Custard Base (page 28) or Eggless Base (page 30)

¼ cup Maker's Mark bourbon

SOUTHERN BELLE ICE CREAM

MAKES ABOUT: 1½ quarts | **ACTIVE TIME:** 50 to 60 minutes

Think boozy peach cobbler, with syrupy-sweet peaches and pecans that highlight the Maker's Mark bourbon.

1   Preheat oven to 325 degrees. Butter a baking sheet.

2   In a large skillet, melt butter and 4 tablespoons of brown sugar together over high heat. Cook until mixture becomes a thick, melted caramel, about 8 to 10 minutes. Deglaze pan with reserved peach juice, whisking until smooth. Bring to a boil and cook for 1 to 2 minutes to reduce slightly, then add peaches and cook until well caramelized, about 5 minutes.

3   With a slotted spoon, lift out peaches and transfer to a bowl. Discard any remaining mixture in pan. Refrigerate.

4   In a small saucepan, bring 2 cups of water to a boil. Add pecans and boil for 5 minutes; they will look waxy. Drain pecans and transfer to a bowl. With a rubber spatula, toss pecans with salt and remaining 2 tablespoons brown sugar until well coated.

5   Spread pecans in a single layer on prepared baking sheet and toast in oven, stirring once, until nuts are dry and sugar-encrusted, about 10 minutes. Transfer to a bowl and let cool slightly. Refrigerate until completely cool, then chop into small pieces.

6   Process base in an ice cream maker according to manufacturer's instructions. Add bourbon during last 2 minutes of churning.

7   Transfer to a bowl and fold in peaches and pecans.

8   Scrape into an airtight storage container. Freeze for a minimum of 2 hours before serving.

WHISKEY LUCKY CHARMS ICE CREAM

MAKES ABOUT: 1½ quarts | **ACTIVE TIME:** 15 to 20 minutes

This milky, fruity concoction, a bottom-of-the-cereal-bowl gem, is sharpened with Irish whiskey and smoothed with sugary marshmallows. Touches of orange blossom, sherry, honey, and vanilla come from the whiskey. It's a grown-up treat that'll make you feel like a kid.

1 Process base in an ice cream maker according to manufacturer's instructions. Add whiskey during last 2 minutes of churning.

2 Transfer to a bowl and fold in cereal.

3 Scrape into an airtight storage container. Freeze for a minimum of 2 hours before serving.

SUGGESTED COOKIE:

Maple Flapjack (page 200)

Plain Custard Base (page 28) or Eggless Base (page 30)

¼ cup Bushmills or Jameson Irish whiskey

¾ cup Lucky Charms cereal

CAKEY

STRAWBERRY COBBLER ICE CREAM

MAKES ABOUT: 1½ quarts | **ACTIVE TIME:** 80 to 90 minutes

An à la mode favorite, with a light and floral flavor. The buttery crumble adds a rich, deeply round texture to this ice cream.

1 Preheat oven to 350 degrees.

2 Mix cornstarch and ½ cup of sugar in a small bowl. Toss with strawberries to coat evenly. Stir in lemon juice and salt. Place in a 9-by-13-inch baking pan. Set aside for about 30 minutes.

3 In a small bowl, combine remaining ½ cup sugar and flour. Drizzle with melted butter and mix to combine. Distribute topping evenly over strawberry mixture in baking dish.

4 Bake until bubbly and topping is golden brown, 45 to 50 minutes.

5 Let cool to room temperature, then refrigerate until cold, about 1 hour.

6 Process base in an ice cream maker according to manufacturer's instructions.

7 Transfer to a bowl. With a wooden spoon, break up cooled strawberry crumble, then fold into ice cream.

8 Scrape into an airtight storage container. Freeze for a minimum of 2 hours before serving.

SUGGESTED COOKIE:

Double Chocolate Sea Salt (page 190)

2 tablespoons cornstarch

1 cup granulated sugar

3 cups hulled, sliced fresh or frozen strawberries (Earthbound Farm and Safeway Organic are good frozen brands)

Juice of 1 lemon (about ¼ cup)

Pinch kosher salt

1 cup sifted all-purpose flour (sift before measuring)

8 tablespoons (1 stick) butter, melted

Plain Custard Base (page 28) or Eggless Base (page 30)

SUGGESTED COOKIES:

Double Chocolate (page 188) or Red Velvet (page 204)

Chocolate Custard Base (page 29)

6 Double Chocolate Cookies (page 188; see Note), broken into ½- to ¾-inch pieces or to taste

NOTE:

Be sure not to overbake the cookies; the centers should be gooey for this ice cream.

MOLTEN CHOCOLATE CAKE ICE CREAM

MAKES ABOUT: 1½ quarts | **ACTIVE TIME:** 50 to 60 minutes

Best summed up in one word: decadent. This is the flavor that you reward yourself with when you've done something good. Something really, really good. It's intense, rich, and pleasantly bitter, with tantalizingly gooey cookies.

1 Process base in an ice cream maker according to manufacturer's instructions.

2 Transfer to a bowl. Gently fold cookie pieces into ice cream.

3 Scrape into an airtight storage container. Freeze for a minimum of 2 hours before serving.

RED VELVET ICE CREAM

MAKES ABOUT: 1½ quarts | **ACTIVE TIME:** 25 to 35 minutes

We think the best part of a red velvet cake is the cheesy, salty frosting—it's soul-strokingly alluring. Think of this ice cream as that frosting, with chunks of crunchy crimson cookies inside.

1 Stir cream cheese, mascarpone, and salt into base with an immersion blender or hand mixer. Mix well.

2 Process in an ice cream maker according to manufacturer's instructions.

3 Transfer to a bowl. Fold cookie chunks into ice cream.

4 Scrape into an airtight storage container. Freeze for a minimum of 2 hours before serving.

SUGGESTED COOKIE:

Red Velvet (page 204)

¼ cup cream cheese, at room temperature

¼ cup mascarpone

Pinch kosher salt

Plain Custard Base (page 28)

6 Red Velvet Cookies (page 204), broken into chunks

CHEESY

HEADS UP: Ice creams with cheese have an increased fat content. Since fats freeze easily, beware of overfreezing when churning.

QUICK FIX: Melt the overfrozen ice cream in the microwave in 30-second zaps until completely liquid, then blend with an immersion blender or a hand mixer, and refreeze. This fix works only once. If you overfreeze the ice cream again, it's garbage.

MASCARPONE FIG ALMOND ICE CREAM

MAKES ABOUT: 1½ quarts | **ACTIVE TIME:** 50 to 60 minutes

SUGGESTED COOKIE:

Oatmeal Raisin (page 191)

The French electronic band Justice chose this flavor to represent them at Coachella. The elegant European flavors of this ice cream get a sugar slap from dried figs, mellowed by mascarpone. The chewiness of the figs contrasts nicely with the crunchy almonds, which add a toasty facet to the ice cream that will make you wanna D-A-N-C-E.

1 cup dry red wine

½ cup granulated sugar

2 whole cloves

Pinch ground nutmeg

4 ounces dried Mission figs, chopped

4 ounces slivered almonds (about ¼ cup)

4 ounces mascarpone

Pinch kosher salt

Plain Custard Base (page 28) or Eggless Base (page 30)

1 In a heavy saucepan, combine wine, sugar, cloves, and nutmeg and bring to a boil over high heat. Reduce heat to low and cook until slightly thickened, about 15 minutes. Add figs and simmer until they are infused with syrup, about 10 minutes. Using a slotted spoon, remove figs from syrup and transfer to a small bowl. Pick out and discard cloves and any syrup. Let figs cool slightly, then refrigerate until ready to use.

2 Preheat oven to 325 degrees.

3 Spread almonds in an even layer on a baking sheet. Toast in oven for 5 to 10 minutes, or until fragrant and golden. Remove from oven and let cool.

4 Mix mascarpone and salt into base using an immersion blender or a hand mixer.

5 Process in an ice cream maker according to manufacturer's instructions.

6 Transfer to a bowl and fold in figs and almonds.

7 Scrape into an airtight container. Freeze for a minimum of 2 hours before serving.

Oatmeal Raisin (page 191) or Maple Flapjack (page 200)

4 ounces cream cheese, cut into ¼-inch squares

Pinch kosher salt

Plain Custard Base (page 28), prepared up to refrigerating step

1 cup orange juice

2 tablespoons cornstarch

¼ cup plus 2 tablespoons granulated sugar

½ pound fresh ripe cherries, stemmed and pitted, or frozen sour pie cherries or Amarena cherries

1 cup graham cracker crumbs

3 tablespoons butter, melted

CHERRY CHEESECAKE ICE CREAM

MAKES ABOUT: 1½ quarts | **ACTIVE TIME:** 40 to 50 minutes

This grown-up recipe features full-on dairy. It's got texture, it's got tang, and if you use the syrupy Italian Amarena dark cherries, it has a sour, lip-smacking richness that cozies up to the cheese. It's the kind of ice cream to enjoy with a full-bodied red wine.

1 With an immersion blender or hand mixer, mix cream cheese and salt into base. Refrigerate as directed.

2 In a heavy saucepan, bring orange juice to a boil over high heat.

3 Mix cornstarch and 2 tablespoons of sugar in a small bowl, then whisk into orange juice. Cook until thickened, stirring occasionally, about 10 minutes. Add cherries. Cook, stirring occasionally, until cherries are slightly softened and well covered with thickened sauce and mixture no longer tastes starchy, about 5 minutes. Remove from heat and let cool slightly.

4 Preheat oven to 350 degrees. Line a baking sheet with parchment paper.

5 Mix together graham crumbs, remaining ¼ cup sugar, and butter. Pack into an even layer onto baking sheet. Toast in oven for 5 to 7 minutes, until lightly browned. Cool.

6 Process base in an ice cream maker according to manufacturer's instructions.

7 Transfer to a bowl and fold in cherry mixture. Break cooled graham cracker crust into pieces and fold into ice cream.

8 Scrape into an airtight storage container. Freeze for a minimum of 2 hours before serving.

BALSAMIC FIG MASCARPONE ICE CREAM

MAKES ABOUT: 1½ quarts | **ACTIVE TIME:** 40 to 45 minutes

This flavor was born from the memory of an appetizer: arugula, flattened dates, prosciutto, and Parmesan baked until the cheese melted. Here we have a frozen, melty cheese plate—without the arugula (too bitter!). Sour and sweet from the balsamic, with just a tickle of acid, the ice cream has a velvety texture from the mellow mascarpone. Sugary figs contribute pleasant chewiness, evoking the Mediterranean.

1 In a small heavy saucepan, bring vinegar and sugar to a boil over high heat and cook until reduced by half. Reduce heat to low, add figs, and reduce liquid until syrup just covers figs, about 20 minutes. Remove from heat and set aside to cool.

2 Mix mascarpone and salt into base with an immersion blender or a hand mixer.

3 Process in an ice cream maker according to manufacturer's instructions.

4 Transfer to a bowl and fold in balsamic-fig mixture.

5 Scrape into an airtight storage container. Freeze for a minimum of 2 hours before serving.

SUGGESTED COOKIES:

Gluten-Free Coconut Almond Chocolate Chip (page 214) or Oatmeal Raisin (page 191)

COOLHAUS SANDWICH CREATION:

Eric Owen Moss-carpone: Oatmeal Raisin Cookies + Balsamic Fig Mascarpone Ice Cream (see Building the Perfect Sandwich, page 25)

1 cup balsamic vinegar

½ cup granulated sugar

1 cup coarsely chopped dried Mission figs

1 (4-ounce) container mascarpone

Pinch kosher salt

Plain Custard Base (page 28) or Eggless Base (page 30)

WHO IS
ERIC OWEN MOSS?

Eric Owen Moss's architectural firm, Eric Owen Moss Architects, has won many awards internationally. His claim to fame: reinvigorating space for commercial use and as performance venues and spiffing up Culver City, California, where we have a Coolhaus shop. A fan of deconstruction and revitalization, Moss also has his own furniture line.

STYLE: Progressive

MAJOR WORKS: Samitaur Tower, and Stealth, Culver City, California; Central Housing Office, University of California, Irvine; Queens Museum of Art, New York City

WHY WE LOVE HIM: He is a UCLA alum (like Natasha) and an L.A. native (like the two of us). His impact on Culver City has breathed new life into its look and economy.

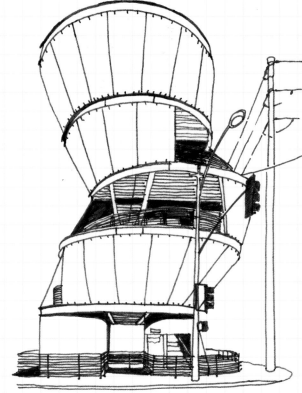

Samitaur Tower

Stealth

NUTTY

SUGGESTED COOKIE:

Snack Food Chocolate Chip (page 210)

¾ cup hazelnuts

2 cups whole milk

2 cups heavy cream

1¼ cups granulated sugar

8 large egg yolks

1 Kit Kat candy bar, chopped or broken into ½- to ¾-inch pieces or to taste

KIT KAT ICE CREAM

MAKES ABOUT: 1½ quarts | **ACTIVE TIME:** 20 to 30 minutes

The ultra-smooth chocolate-hazelnut base makes this ice cream super-creamy. Add the crunch of Kit Kats and you've got the perfect fix for the munchies, though it's a little more refined than your classic stoner flavors.

We made this flavor for Coachella for the Grammy Award—winning garage rock band the Black Keys. Think about it: Kit Kats equal edible black piano keys!

1 Preheat oven to 325 degrees.

2 Spread hazelnuts in a single layer on a baking sheet. Toast in oven for 5 to 10 minutes, or until fragrant and golden. Remove from oven and let cool. Smash into pieces.

3 In a 4-quart saucepan, combine the milk, cream, and half of sugar and bring to a boil over medium-high heat. Meanwhile, beat yolks and remaining sugar until smooth, heavy, and pale yellow, about 30 seconds.

4 When cream mixture boils, add toasted hazelnuts, remove from heat, and let stand for 10 minutes. Strain cream mixture through a fine-mesh sieve into a bowl. Transfer hazelnuts to a blender and puree, adding a bit of cream mixture to help pureeing process.

5 Strain pureed hazelnuts through a fine-mesh sieve into bowl with remaining cream mixture and return liquid to saucepan. Discard any solids left in sieve.

6 In a slow stream, pour half of cream mixture over yolk-sugar mixture, whisking constantly until blended.

7 Return pan to stovetop over low heat. Whisking constantly, stream yolk-cream mixture back into pan.

8   With a wooden spoon, continue stirring until mixture registers 165 to 180 degrees on an instant-read thermometer, about 2 minutes. Do not heat above 180 degrees, or eggs in base will scramble. Mixture should be slightly thickened and coat back of spoon, with steam rising, but not boiling. (If you blow on the back of the spoon and the mixture ripples, you've got the right consistency.)

9   Pour into a clean airtight container and refrigerate for 12 to 24 hours.

10 Process in an ice cream maker according to manufacturer's instructions.

11 Transfer to a bowl and stir in Kit Kat pieces.

12 Scrape into an airtight storage container. Freeze for a minimum of 2 hours before serving.

NUTELLA TOASTED ALMOND ICE CREAM

MAKES ABOUT: 1½ quarts | **ACTIVE TIME:** 50 to 55 minutes

Toasted almonds give an extra twist to the hazelnut essence of this ice cream.

1 Preheat oven to 325 degrees.

2 Spread hazelnuts in a single layer on a baking sheet. Toast in oven for 5 to 10 minutes, or until fragrant and golden. Remove from oven and let cool. Smash into pieces.

3 In a 4-quart saucepan, combine milk, cream, and half of sugar and bring to a boil over medium-high heat. Meanwhile, beat yolks and remaining sugar until smooth, heavy, and pale yellow, about 30 seconds.

4 When cream mixture boils, add toasted hazelnuts, remove from heat, and let stand for 10 minutes. Strain cream mixture through a fine-mesh sieve into a bowl. Transfer hazelnuts to a blender and puree, adding a bit of cream mixture to help pureeing process.

5 Strain pureed hazelnuts through a fine-mesh sieve into bowl with remaining cream mixture and return liquid to saucepan. Discard any solids left in sieve.

6 In a slow stream, pour half of cream mixture over yolk-sugar mixture, whisking constantly until blended.

7 Return pan to stovetop over low heat. Whisking constantly, stream yolk-cream mixture back into pan.

SUGGESTED COOKIES:

Pretzel Chocolate Chunk (page 202) or S'mores (page 209)

COOLHAUS SANDWICH CREATION:

David Rocky Roadwell: S'mores Cookies + Nutella Toasted Almond Ice Cream (see Building the Perfect Sandwich, page 25)

¾ cup hazelnuts

2 cups whole milk

2 cups heavy cream

1¼ cups granulated sugar

8 large egg yolks

½ cup sliced almonds (with skins)

Maldon sea salt, for sprinkling

RECIPE CONTINUES

8   With a wooden spoon, continue stirring until mixture registers 165 to 180 degrees on an instant-read thermometer, about 2 minutes. Do not heat above 180 degrees, or eggs in base will scramble. Mixture should be slightly thickened and coat back of spoon, with steam rising, but not boiling. (If you blow on the back of the spoon and the mixture ripples, you've got the right consistency.)

9   Pour into a clean airtight container and refrigerate for 12 to 24 hours.

10 Process in an ice cream maker according to manufacturer's instructions.

11 Meanwhile, preheat oven to 325 degrees.

12 Spread almonds in a single layer on a baking sheet. Toast in oven for 5 to 10 minutes, or until fragrant and golden. Remove from oven and let cool.

13 Transfer churned ice cream to a bowl and stir in toasted almonds.

14 Scrape into an airtight storage container. Freeze for a minimum of 2 hours before serving.

15 Top with a sprinkling of sea salt.

WHO IS DAVID ROCKWELL?

An American architect and designer, David Rockwell grew up in Chicago, New Jersey, and Mexico. His flair for the dramatic came from his upbringing by his dancer-choreographer mother. Rockwell's work spans restaurants, hotels, theaters, and set design, including backdrops for Broadway productions and the Academy Awards.

STYLE: Modern, ornate, colorful

MAJOR WORKS: The Cosmopolitan of Las Vegas; the Walt Disney Family Museum, San Francisco; five Nobu restaurants; interior design for JetBlue Airways terminal, John F. Kennedy International Airport, New York City

WHY WE LOVE HIM: We heart Rockwell's drama, especially in set designs, such as the Broadway revival of *The Rocky Horror Picture Show*. Rockwell's New York City office was one of many places we served this flavor after Hurricane Sandy—our New York City trucks doubled as emergency relief vehicles after the storm.

PEANUT BUTTER ICE CREAM

MAKES ABOUT: 1½ quarts | **ACTIVE TIME:** 20 to 25 minutes

We probably never argued over an ice cream like we did with this. Freya wanted to use crunchy peanut butter, while Natasha wanted creamy. In the end, creamy won.

Peanut butter makes the perfect salty, savory partner for the sweet custard base. The best part about it is that it takes to all manner of stir-ins: It provides a great canvas for brownie chunks, broken cookies, grape jelly, chocolate chips—even curry or candied bacon bits.

Because of the peanut butter, the quantity of cream is reduced, and adding ¼ cup more sugar ensures that the peanut butter doesn't set too firmly once the ice cream is frozen.

1 In a 4-quart saucepan, combine milk, cream, and half of sugar and bring to a boil over medium-high heat. Meanwhile, beat yolks and remaining sugar until smooth, heavy, and pale yellow, about 30 seconds.

2 When cream mixture comes to a boil, in a slow stream, pour half of cream mixture over yolk-sugar mixture, whisking constantly until blended.

3 Return pan to stovetop over low heat. Whisking constantly, stream yolk-cream mixture back into pan.

RECIPE CONTINUES

SUGGESTED COOKIES:

Double Chocolate (page 188), Peanut Butter with Cap'n Crunch (page 206), or Snickerdoodle (page 194)

COOLHAUS SANDWICH CREATION:

I. M. Pei-nut Butter: Double Chocolate Cookie + Peanut Butter Ice Cream (see Building the Perfect Sandwich, page 25)

3 cups whole milk

1 cup heavy cream

1½ cups granulated sugar

8 large egg yolks

4 ounces (½ cup) natural peanut butter (we like brands made with Valencia peanuts), at room temperature

1 teaspoon kosher salt

4 With a wooden spoon, continue stirring until mixture registers 165 to 180 degrees on an instant-read thermometer, about 2 minutes. Do not heat above 180 degrees, or eggs in base will scramble. Mixture should be slightly thickened and coat back of spoon, with steam rising, but not boiling. (If you blow on the back of the spoon and the mixture ripples, you've got the right consistency.)

5 Pour into a clean airtight container and refrigerate for 12 to 24 hours.

6 Mix peanut butter and salt into base with an immersion blender or a hand mixer.

7 Process in an ice cream maker according to manufacturer's instructions.

8 Scrape into an airtight storage container. Freeze for a minimum of 2 hours before serving.

TRY THIS:

For Peanut Butter Curry Ice Cream, add 1 tablespoon curry. For Peanut Butter and Jelly Ice Cream, add ¼ cup grape jelly. To create your own peanut butter flavor, add ½ cup of your favorite stir-in (cookie chunks, brownie chunks, candied bacon bits, chocolate chips). For all add-ins, transfer churned ice cream to a bowl and stir in before scraping into the airtight storage container and freezing.

WHO IS I . M . PEI?

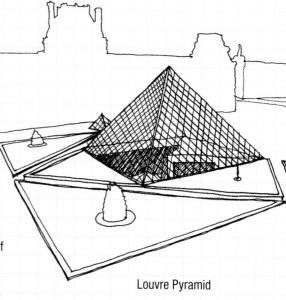

Louvre Pyramid

Born in China, schooled at the University of Pennsylvania, MIT, and Harvard, I. M. Pei is one of the world's most prolific architects. His distinctive modernist work grew out of his schooling in, and dislike for, the modern decorative Beaux-Arts movement. During World War II, he volunteered for the National Defense Research Committee, a weapons technology think tank.

STYLE: Modernist with cubist influence

MAJOR WORKS: John F. Kennedy Presidential Library and Museum, Boston; Bank of China Tower, Hong Kong; Louvre Pyramid, Paris

WHY WE LOVE HIM: His sons Didi and Sandi followed in his footsteps and are also architects. (Natasha followed in her dad's footsteps, too, by studying architecture.) He's a nonagenarian. His distinctive geometric forms are recognizable the world over.

PISTACHIO BLACK TRUFFLE ICE CREAM

MAKES ABOUT: 1½ quarts | **ACTIVE TIME:** 30 to 35 minutes

If you combine the wonderful taste of roasty, salty pistachios with the delicate sweetness of our base and the deep, earthy aromatics of black truffle oil, you get an explosion of taste. Because of its perfect sweet, salty, and savory balance, pistachio gelato is considered to be the best in Italy.

A few myths busted: Pistachio ice cream should not be bright green; it should have a faint yellow-olive color. And it should taste nothing like those nuclear-green brands.

1 Preheat oven to 350 degrees.

2 Spread pistachio nuts in a single layer on a baking sheet, sprinkle with 1 pinch of salt, and toast in oven for 10 to 12 minutes, until aromatic.

3 Stir nuts (preferably still warm) into hot base. Let base cool slightly, then pour into a blender and puree until smooth. Add with remaining pinch of salt.

4 Pour into a clean airtight container. Refrigerate for 12 to 24 hours.

5 Mix black truffle oil into base, then process in an ice cream maker according to manufacturer's instructions.

6 Scrape into an airtight storage container. Freeze for a minimum of 2 hours before serving.

SUGGESTED COOKIE:

Oatmeal Raisin (page 191)

½ cup shelled unsalted pistachio nuts

2 pinches sea salt

Plain Custard Base (page 28), prepared up to refrigerating step, still hot

1 teaspoon black truffle oil (see Sources, page 23)

SALTY

SALTED CARAMEL ICE CREAM

MAKES ABOUT: 1½ quarts | **ACTIVE TIME:** 15 to 20 minutes

Salt sets off the über-sweetness of caramel while playing up the butterscotch notes in this ice cream.

1 In a 4-quart saucepan, combine milk and cream and heat over medium-high heat until just before boiling. Set aside.

2 Meanwhile, beat yolks and half of sugar with a whisk until smooth, heavy, and pale yellow, about 30 seconds.

3 Heat a large, heavy saucepan over medium-high heat. When hot, sprinkle remaining sugar into pan by the spoonful. As each spoonful melts, add another and gently mix with a long-handled whisk or wooden spoon. Repeat until all sugar is used.

4 The sugar will begin caramelizing very soon. The color will go from pale to golden to amber to dark. (Don't panic! The color needs to be dark for the ice cream to have flavor.) When the bubbles get foamy and smoke rises, remove pan from heat. (Do not allow caramel to burn.)

5 Whisk a small amount of hot cream mixture into caramelized sugar. Be careful: It will steam up and bubble. Keep adding cream mixture, whisking, until it is all incorporated.

6 Return pan to medium-high heat and gently bring mixture to a boil. Whisk to gently incorporate any hardened "rocks" or pieces of caramel sticking to side of pan.

7 When caramel-cream mixture comes to a boil, in a slow stream, pour half of cream mixture over yolk-sugar mixture, whisking constantly until blended.

8 Return pan to stovetop over low heat. Whisking constantly, stream yolk-cream mixture back into pan.

SUGGESTED COOKIE:

Snickerdoodle (page 194) or Double Chocolate Sea Salt (page 190)

COOLHAUS SANDWICH CREATION:

Caramia Lehrer: Snickerdoodle Cookies + Salted Caramel Ice Cream (see Building the Perfect Sandwich, page 25)

2 cups whole milk

2 cups heavy cream

8 large egg yolks

1¼ cups granulated sugar

1 tablespoon sea salt (such as Maldon or fleur de sel)

RECIPE CONTINUES

9 With a wooden spoon, continue stirring until mixture registers 165 to 180 degrees on an instant-read thermometer, about 2 minutes. Do not heat above 180 degrees, or eggs in base will scramble. Mixture should be slightly thickened and coat back of spoon, with steam rising, but not boiling. (If you blow on the back of the spoon and the mixture ripples, you've got the right consistency.)

10 Transfer to a bowl and mix with an immersion blender or a hand mixer. Mix in sea salt.

11 Pour into to a clean airtight container and refrigerate for 12 to 24 hours.

12 Process in an ice cream maker according to manufacturer's instructions.

13 Scrape into an airtight storage container. Freeze for a minimum of 2 hours before serving.

WHO IS MIA LEHRER?

Originally from El Salvador, Harvard University Graduate School of Design alum Mia Lehrer is now the principal of her own landscape architectural firm. Her designs feature innovative solutions for water conservation and environmental preservation. She also has a penchant for found objects and architectural planters.

STYLE: Progressive landscape architecture

MAJOR WORKS: Vista Hermosa Park, Los Angeles; World Bank Coastal Zone Project, El Salvador; Union Station, Los Angeles

WHY WE LOVE HER: She claims Frederick L. Olmstead, the designer of New York City's Central Park, as one of her major inspirations. She's a close Case family friend, she is one of the most established landscape architects in the world, and she is our hero and always an inspiration.

Vista Hermosa Park

SUGGESTED COOKIES:

Pretzel Chocolate Chunk (page 202), Red Velvet (page 204), or Gluten-Free Coconut Almond Chocolate Chip (page 214)

COOLHAUS SANDWICH CREATION:

Jennifer's Joy: Gluten-Free Coconut Almond Chocolate Chip Cookies + Salted Chocolate Almond Joy Ice Cream (see Building the Perfect Sandwich, page 25)

Chocolate Custard Base (page 29), with 1 tablespoon Maldon sea salt or fleur de sel added with chocolate

½ cup broken Almond Joy candy bar

Sea salt, for sprinkling

SALTED CHOCOLATE ALMOND JOY ICE CREAM

MAKES ABOUT: 1½ quarts | **ACTIVE TIME:** 15 to 20 minutes

We love using Maldon sea salt because a little sprinkling over each serving adds a nice crunchy texture. The Maldon plays up the savory notes of cacao as opposed to the sweet. The resulting flavor is sophisticated, refined, and grown-up.

1. Process base in an ice cream maker according to manufacturer's instructions.

2. Transfer to a bowl and fold in candy pieces.

3. Scrape into an airtight storage container. Freeze for a minimum of 2 hours before serving.

4. Top with a sprinkle of sea salt.

WHO IS

JENNIFER SIEGAL?

Founder of Office of Mobile Design (OMD), Jennifer Siegal has created what she calls the "Prefab home of the twenty-first century." She is the editor of the Princeton Architectural Press publications *Mobile: The Art of Portable Architecture* and *More Mobile: Portable Architecture for Today*, and was founder and editor of *Materials Monthly*.

STYLE: Portable and sustainable modernist

MAJOR WORKS: Mobile ECO LAB, Los Angeles; Portable Construction Training Center for Venice Community Housing Corporation, Venice, California

WHY WE LOVE HER: Jennifer put herself through school using the proceeds from her hot dog cart. As a company that started on a food truck, we're huge groupies of someone who is all about mobile architecture.

Mobile ECO LAB

WHITE CHOCOLATE & OLIVE ICE CREAM

MAKES ABOUT: 1½ quarts | **ACTIVE TIME:** 15 to 20 minutes

The white chocolate is a little floral, and the Kalamata olives (our favorite kind) bring in a little brininess, with a surprising hint of vanilla.

1. Process base in an ice cream maker according to manufacturer's instructions.

2. Transfer to a bowl and fold in olives.

3. Scrape into an airtight storage container. Freeze for a minimum of 2 hours before serving.

4. Top with a sprinkling of sea salt.

SUGGESTED COOKIE:

Double Chocolate Sea Salt (page 190)

Chocolate Custard Base (page 29), made with 6 ounces (¾ cup chopped) white chocolate (we like Callebaut) instead of bittersweet

½ cup chopped Kalamata olives

Maldon sea salt, for sprinkling

SAVORY

PEKING DUCK ICE CREAM

MAKES ABOUT: 1½ quarts | **ACTIVE TIME:** 35 to 40 minutes

This flavor occurred to us while eating out at our favorite Chinese restaurant. Salty and crispy meets the aromatic blend of five-spice powder, with its notes of star anise, clove, fennel, cinnamon, and black pepper. A sweet swirl of hoisin sauce evens out the duck drippings. Don't wait for Chinese New Year to enjoy this sugary-savory ice cream.

1 Preheat oven to 400 degrees.

2 Place julienned duck skin on a baking sheet and roast for 5 to 10 minutes, or until fat is rendered. Reserve 1 teaspoon rendered duck fat. Set skin aside to cool.

3 Add reserved duck fat to base and stir to incorporate.

4 Process in an ice cream maker according to manufacturer's instructions.

5 Transfer to a bowl and swirl in hoisin sauce (see tips, page 24). Fold in roasted duck skin.

6 Scrape into an airtight storage container. Freeze for a minimum of 2 hours before serving.

7 Top with a sprinkling of smashed fortune cookies.

SUGGESTED COOKIES:

Snickerdoodle (page 194), Maple Flapjack (page 200), or Double Chocolate Sea Salt (page 190)

Crispy skin from 1 plain roast Peking duck (ordered from your favorite Chinese restaurant), sliced julienne-style into strips

Plain Custard Base (page 28), with 1 tablespoon Chinese five-spice powder added to cream mixture before heating

3 to 4 tablespoons Lee Kum Kee hoisin sauce

4 fortune cookies, fortunes removed, smashed into pieces, for serving

---

SUGGESTED COOKIES:

Double Chocolate Sea Salt (page 190) or
Snickerdoodle (page 194)

2 cups whole milk

2 cups heavy cream

1¼ cups granulated sugar

8 large egg yolks

11 ounces raw foie gras, deveined
and cleaned

¼ cup honey

12 whole peppercorns, coarsely
broken or crushed with the side of
a chef's knife, plus a grinding of
black pepper (optional)

½ cup sherry vinegar

FOIE GRAS ICE CREAM

MAKES ABOUT: 1½ quarts | **ACTIVE TIME:** 35 to 45 minutes

Foie gras provides a wonderful silky texture and opulence to the base. All that richness needs some acidity and sweetness to balance it, and that's where our sherry-honey—black pepper *gastrique* comes in—a powerful, pleasantly pungent counterpoint that turns up the luxurious liver-y edge in the ice cream. This is our Michelin-starred flavor.

1 In a 4-quart saucepan, combine milk, cream, and half of sugar and bring to a boil over high heat.

2 Meanwhile, beat yolks and remaining sugar with a whisk until smooth, heavy, and pale yellow.

3 When cream mixture comes to a boil, reduce heat to low, add foie gras, and poach in hot mixture until an instant-read thermometer inserted into foie gras registers 135 degrees, 8 to 10 minutes. Do not overpoach, or foie gras will become crumbly. Remove from heat and let cool for about 5 minutes.

4 Pour half of cooled foie-cream mixture into a blender. Starting on low speed and working up to high, blend until smooth. Strain pureed foie mixture through a fine-mesh sieve into a clean saucepan. Repeat with remaining foie-cream mixture.

5 Whisk pureed foie mixture in saucepan. Bring mixture to a boil over medium-low heat. When mixture just comes to a boil, in a slow stream, pour half of foie mixture over yolk-sugar mixture, whisking constantly until blended.

6 Return pan to stovetop over low heat. Whisking constantly, stream yolk-foie mixture back into pan.

7 With a wooden spoon, continue stirring until mixture registers 165 to 180 degrees on an instant-read thermometer, about 2 minutes. Do not heat above 180 degrees, or eggs in base will scramble. Mixture should be slightly thickened and coat back of spoon, with steam rising, but not boiling. (If you blow on the back of the spoon and the mixture ripples, you've got the right consistency.)

8 Pour into a clean airtight container and refrigerate for 12 to 24 hours.

9 Process in an ice cream maker according to manufacturer's instructions.

10 Meanwhile, make sherry-honey–black pepper *gastrique:* In a heavy 2-quart saucepan, combine honey and peppercorns and cook over high heat until honey caramelizes (this will happen quickly—it will sputter, get foamy, and give off a little smoke), 1 to 2 minutes.

11 Carefully whisk in sherry vinegar. Bring to a boil, reduce heat to low, and gently simmer until reduced to a syrup, about 15 minutes.

12 With a slotted spoon, remove and discard peppercorns. Let syrup cool.

13 Transfer ice cream to a bowl and swirl in *gastrique* (see tips, page 24). Add a final grinding of fresh black pepper, if you wish.

14 Scrape into an airtight storage container. Freeze for a minimum of 2 hours before serving.

TIP:

Foie gras cubes from D'Artagnan (www .dartagnan.com) work well for this recipe and are not too costly. If purchasing foie gras from the market, ask for grade B for great flavor at a lower cost.

SUGGESTED COOKIES:

Maple Flapjack (page 200) or Chocolate Chip (page 187)

1 cup Fried Chicken Caramel (page 229)

4 tablespoons (½ stick) unsalted butter

Plain Custard Base (page 28)

1 cup smashed waffle cookies (Pirouette cookies, Breton fan cookies, or organic waffle cones)

FRIED CHICKEN & WAFFLE ICE CREAM

MAKES ABOUT: 1½ quarts | **ACTIVE TIME:** 2 to 2½ hours

We started to wonder, What would be our next sensation, the equivalent of our Brown Butter Candied Bacon Ice Cream (page 68)? That's when we came up with this down-home, salty, sweet, Southern, finger-lickin'-great concoction. The brown butter base is enhanced with an herbaceous, slightly spiced Fried Chicken Caramel dotted with crispy skin—definitely one of Coolhaus's unique triumphs. In fact, the caramel, which is sold in our signature Coolhaus jars, is one of our best sellers. Make it on its own and serve it over anything.

1 Refrigerate the caramel for 30 minutes. Mix with an immersion blender or a hand mixer to emulsify.

2 In a small saucepan, melt butter over medium heat and cook until medium-brown/caramel in color, about 4 minutes. Be careful not to burn. Remove from heat and strain through a fine-mesh sieve into a small bowl. Let cool.

3 Add brown butter to base. Stir to combine.

4 Process in an ice cream maker according to manufacturer's instructions. During last minute of churning, swirl in caramel.

5 Transfer to a bowl and fold in smashed waffle cookies.

6 Scrape into an airtight storage container. Freeze for a minimum of 2 hours before serving.

SUGGESTED COOKIES:

Lemon Pine Nut Rosemary (page 198) or Snickerdoodle (page 194)

3 cups whole milk

1 cup heavy cream

1¼ cups granulated sugar

2 (4-inch) sprigs fresh rosemary

8 large egg yolks

½ cup fruity extra-virgin olive oil, plus more for drizzling

Maldon sea salt or fleur de sel, for sprinkling

OLIVE OIL & ROSEMARY ICE CREAM

MAKES ABOUT: 1½ quarts | **ACTIVE TIME:** 20 to 25 minutes

We enjoy eating at Mario Batali's Los Angeles restaurant, Osteria Mozza, where there's a terrific olive oil—rosemary cake on the menu. This is our translation of that dessert into ice cream. Rosemary is the star, but the fruitiness of olive oil quiets the herbaceousness of the rosemary so that each partner gives a great supporting performance.

Use a fruity extra-virgin olive oil. The reduced amount of cream in the base reflects the addition of the olive oil. The resulting texture is nice and velvety.

1 In a 4-quart saucepan, combine milk, cream, half of sugar, and rosemary sprigs. Set over high heat, and cook, stirring occasionally, until mixture comes to a boil, about 5 minutes.

2 Meanwhile, in a medium bowl, whisk yolks and remaining sugar until smooth, heavy, and pale yellow, about 30 seconds.

3 When cream mixture just comes to a boil, whisk, remove from heat, and, in a slow stream, pour half of cream mixture over yolk-sugar mixture, whisking constantly until blended.

4 Return pan to stovetop over low heat. Whisking constantly, stream yolk-cream mixture back into pan.

5 With a wooden spoon, continue stirring until mixture registers 165 to 180 degrees on an instant-read thermometer, about 2 minutes. Do not heat above 180 degrees, or eggs in base will scramble. Mixture should be slightly thickened and coat back of spoon, with steam rising, but not boiling. (If you blow on the back of the spoon and the mixture ripples, you've got the right consistency.)

6 Pour into a clean airtight container and refrigerate for 12 to 24 hours.

7 Remove rosemary. Drizzle olive oil into base and mix to incorporate.

8 Process in an ice cream maker according to manufacturer's instructions.

9 Scrape into an airtight storage container. Freeze for a minimum of 2 hours before serving.

10 Top with a drizzle of olive oil and a pinch of sea salt.

SMOKY/
SPICY

CHOCOLATE CHIPOTLE BARBECUE ICE CREAM

MAKES ABOUT: 1½ quarts | **ACTIVE TIME:** 20 to 25 minutes

This flavor was inspired by the famous Franklin Barbecue restaurant in Austin, Texas. Imagine you had just eaten a spice-rubbed, long-smoked brisket doused with a tangy barbecue sauce. Then you plopped some chocolate cake onto the plate. The resulting sweet, smoky, zingy, peppery, perky, tangy blend is truly complex, as only great Texas barbecue can be.

1 Stir pureed chipotle pepper in adobo into cream mixture of base before heating. Proceed as directed.

2 Process in an ice cream maker according to manufacturer's instructions.

3 Transfer to a bowl and swirl in whiskey barbecue sauce (see tips, page 24).

4 Scrape into an airtight storage container. Freeze for a minimum of 2 hours before serving.

SUGGESTED COOKIES:

Red Velvet (page 204), Gluten-Free Coconut Almond Chocolate Chip (page 214), or Snack Food Chocolate Chip (page 210)

1 pureed canned chipotle pepper in adobo (or 1½ peppers, if you like things spicy)

Chocolate Custard Base (page 29)

3 tablespoons whiskey barbecue sauce (such as Lynchburg, Wild Turkey, Stubbs, or Sticky Fingers)

TIP:

You can get whiskey barbecue sauce online from www.stubbsbbq.com or www.hotsauceworld.com.

SUGGESTED COOKIES:

Chocolate Chip (page 187) or Pretzel
Chocolate Chunk (page 202)

**COOLHAUS SANDWICH
CREATION:**

Louis Ba-kahn: Chocolate Chip Cookies +
Brown Butter Candied Bacon Ice Cream
(see Building the Perfect Sandwich,
page 25)

½ stick (4 tablespoons) butter

8 (1-ounce) strips bacon

½ cup maple syrup

½ teaspoon sea salt

Plain Custard Base (page 28)

BROWN BUTTER CANDIED BACON ICE CREAM

MAKES ABOUT: 1½ quarts | **ACTIVE TIME:** 40 to 45 minutes

The teetotaler version of Bourbon Brown Butter
Candied Bacon Ice Cream (page 68), this has the same
salty, smoky, sweet, rich goodness, but without
the boozy edge. Sandwiched between chocolate chip
cookies, it's the center of the knockout sandwich
known as the Louis Ba-kahn, one of our most popular
combinations.

1. In a small saucepan, melt butter over medium heat and cook until it is a medium brown/caramel color, about 4 minutes. Be careful not to burn. Remove from heat and strain through a fine-mesh sieve into a small bowl. Let cool.

2. In a large skillet, cook bacon strips over medium-low heat, turning, until just before crispy. Transfer to paper towels to drain and cool.

3. When cool, finely dice bacon strips. In a clean skillet, combine diced bacon and maple syrup and cook over medium-high heat for about 3 minutes, until syrup is thick and has reduced by half. Sprinkle with sea salt. Remove from heat and set aside to cool.

4. Mix cooled brown butter and candied bacon into base.

5. Process in an ice cream maker according to manufacturer's instructions.

6. Scrape into an airtight storage container. Freeze for a minimum of 2 hours before serving.

WHO IS
LOUIS KAHN?

Born as Itze-Leib Schmuilowsky in Estonia in 1901, this Philadelphia-based architect was an illustrious professor of architecture at Yale University and the University of Pennsylvania and is often hailed as one of the most influential designers of the twentieth century. His work, large and sculpture-like, has a back-to-basics feel.

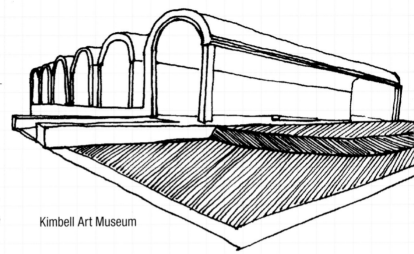

Kimbell Art Museum

STYLE: Postmodern eclectic

MAJOR WORKS: Salk Institute for Biological Studies, La Jolla, California; Franklin D. Roosevelt Four Freedoms Park, Roosevelt Island, New York City; Kimbell Art Museum, Fort Worth, Texas

WHY WE LOVE HIM: He's the subject of the fascinating, Oscar-nominated documentary *My Architect: A Son's Journey*, made by his son, Nathaniel Kahn.

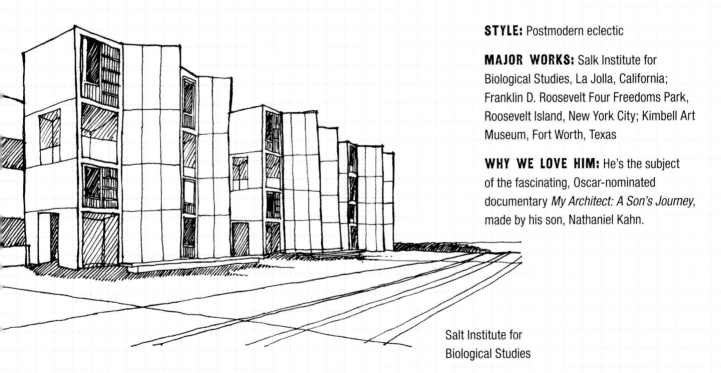

Salt Institute for Biological Studies

CHOCOLATE WASABI ICE CREAM

MAKES ABOUT: 1½ quarts | **ACTIVE TIME:** 20 to 25 minutes

The exotic, horseradish-like punch of wasabi sneaks up on the sweet chocolaty overtones of this surprising flavor, making the mouth sizzle. The ice cream is a natural partner to our Vegan Ginger Molasses Cookies.

1 Whisk wasabi into base.

2 Process in an ice cream maker according to manufacturer's instructions.

3 Scrape into an airtight storage container. Freeze for a minimum of 2 hours before serving.

SUGGESTED COOKIE:

Vegan Ginger Molasses (page 217)

1 teaspoon wasabi paste, or
1 teaspoon wasabi powder
mixed with 2 to 3 teaspoons
cold water

Chocolate Custard Base (page 29)

CUBAN CIGAR ICE CREAM

MAKES ABOUT: 1½ quarts | **ACTIVE TIME:** 20 to 25 minutes

The essences of coffee, chicory, hickory, caramel, and mesquite combine with liquid smoke in this homage to a Cuban cigar. The smoke brings a burn to this flavor. Not surprisingly, the ice cream is a huge hit in our Miami market. Enjoy it after a great meal, when celebrating the birth of a baby boy, or after winning the lottery!

1 Before refrigerating base, stir in coffee powder, salt, and liquid smoke. Refrigerate as directed.

2 Process in an ice cream maker according to manufacturer's instructions.

3 Scrape into an airtight storage container. Freeze for a minimum of 2 hours before serving.

SUGGESTED COOKIES:

Double Chocolate Sea Salt (page 190) or Gluten-Free Coconut Almond Chocolate Chip (page 204)

Salted Caramel Ice Cream base (page 109), prepared up to refrigerating step

1 teaspoon instant coffee powder (such as Folgers)

¼ teaspoon Maldon sea salt or fleur de sel

1 teaspoon Colgin Liquid Smoke (usually found near barbecue sauces in supermarkets)

BEVERAGE-INSPIRED

VEGAN HORCHATA ICE CREAM

MAKES ABOUT: 1 quart | **ACTIVE TIME:** 20 to 25 minutes

Horchata, a Latin American beverage made from almonds, sesame seeds, and rice or barley, is big in L.A.; it's an incredibly refreshing drink found at any taco truck. Ours is Mexican-style, which means it is made with rice milk, so it's vegan-friendly. It's milky, sweet, and cinnamony and tastes like frozen rice pudding.

1 In a 4-quart saucepan, combine sugar, rice milk, honey, kosher salt, and cinnamon. Heat over medium-low heat, stirring occasionally, just until sugar dissolves. Remove from heat and let cool to room temperature.

2 Process in an ice cream maker according to manufacturer's instructions.

3 Scrape into an airtight storage container. Freeze for a minimum of 2 hours before serving.

SUGGESTED COOKIES:

Cinnamon Toast Crunch (page 197) or Snickerdoodle (page 194)

¾ cup granulated sugar

3 cups rice milk

1 tablespoon honey

Pinch kosher salt

¼ teaspoon ground cinnamon

SUGGESTED COOKIE:

Red Velvet (page 204)

COOLHAUS SANDWICH CREATION:

Oreo Heckman: Red Velvet Cookies + Coffee Oreo Ice Cream (see Building the Perfect Sandwich, page 205)

- 2 tablespoons instant coffee powder (such as Folgers)
- Plain Custard Base (page 28), prepared up to refrigerating step
- 6 to 8 Oreo sandwich cookies, chopped or smashed with rolling pin

COFFEE OREO ICE CREAM

MAKES ABOUT: 1½ quarts | **ACTIVE TIME:** 15 to 20 minutes

The bitter nuttiness of coffee and the crunch of deep-chocolate cookie pieces pairs perfectly with our signature creamy base.

1. Stir coffee powder into base to dissolve. Refrigerate base as directed.
2. Process in an ice cream maker according to manufacturer's instructions.
3. Transfer to a bowl and fold in cookie pieces.
4. Scrape into an airtight storage container. Freeze for a minimum of 2 hours before serving.

WHO IS ARI HECKMAN?

Heckman is the founder of the interior design and real estate development firm ASH NYC, as well as the home design shop ASH NYC in Williamsburg, a neighborhood in Brooklyn, New York.

STYLE: ASH NYC is known for the blending of the modern and the vintage and transforming of spaces to defy one era or aesthetic.

MAJOR WORKS: Lobby of 133 Water Street, New York City; whaler's cottage, Sag Harbor, New York; The Dean Hotel, Providence, Rhode Island

WHY WE LOVE HIM: He's a young, vibrant Cornell alum who is making a huge impression on interior design across the country.

SUGGESTED COOKIES:

Snickerdoodle (page 194) or Oatmeal Raisin (page 191)

COOLHAUS SANDWICH CREATION:

Le Corbus-tea-er: Snickerdoodle Cookies + Earl Grey Ice Cream (see Building the Perfect Sandwich, page 25)

Plain Custard Base (page 28)

3 Twinings Earl Grey tea bags

Pinch kosher salt

EARL GREY ICE CREAM

MAKES ABOUT: 1½ quarts | **ACTIVE TIME:** 15 to 20 minutes

This slightly bitter, brightly citrusy, floral, and fragrant ice cream has an exotic finish.

1 In a small saucepan, heat about one quarter of base over low heat, being careful not to let boil. Add tea bags and steep for 5 to 6 minutes. Remove and discard tea bags.

2 Stir tea-infused mixture and salt into remaining base.

3 Process in an ice cream maker according to manufacturer's instructions.

4 Scrape into an airtight storage container. Freeze for a minimum of 2 hours before serving.

Villa Savoye

WHO IS

LE CORBUSIER?

Swiss-French writer, artist, and architect Le Corbusier, a.k.a. Charles-Édouard Jeanneret, took the pseudonym to honor his grandfather (with an altered spelling of the name). His raison d'être was to improve living conditions in overcrowded urban areas. He, with the cubist painter Amédée Ozenfant, established Purism, a postcubist artistic movement.

STYLE: Modernist

MAJOR WORKS: Consultant for United Nations Headquarters, New York City; Villa Savoye, Poissy, France; Saddam Hussein Gymnasium, Baghdad; National Museum of Western Art, Tokyo; Chapelle Notre-Dame-du-Haut, Ronchamp, France

WHY WE LOVE HIM: The dude rolls with a pseudonym. Also, he shacked up with legendary singer-entertainer Josephine Baker.

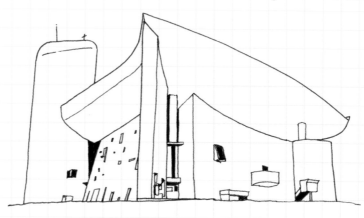

Chapelle Notre-Dame-du-Haut

GREEN TEA ICE CREAM

MAKES ABOUT: 1½ quarts | **ACTIVE TIME:** 15 to 20 minutes

This ice cream is ridiculously easy to make, and it helps ease the digestion after a big meal or some sushi. We use high-quality matcha green tea powder to give the ice cream a vibrant color and an earthy flavor. A little smoky, a little bitter, with some cream and sugar, it's Zen-tastic.

1 Stir matcha powder into base.

2 Process in an ice cream maker according to manufacturer's instructions.

3 Scrape into an airtight storage container. Freeze for a minimum of 2 hours before serving.

SUGGESTED COOKIES:

Vegan Ginger Molasses (page 217) or Double Chocolate (page 188)

COOLHAUS SANDWICH CREATION:

Tea-dao Ando: Vegan Ginger Molasses Cookies + Green Tea Ice Cream (see Building the Perfect Sandwich, page 25)

---

2 tablespoons matcha green tea powder (available at specialy tea shops or www.matchasource.com)

Plain Custard Base (page 28)

WHO IS
TADAO ANDO?

A self-taught Japanese architect, Tadao Ando is known for his creative use of natural light and for building to conform to the natural landscape, instead of vice versa. He has designed dozens of housing complexes throughout Japan.

STYLE: Minimalist/critical regionalism, a reaction to modernism's lack of style

MAJOR WORKS: Church of the Light, Osaka, Japan; Morimoto restaurant interior, New York City; Modern Art Museum of Fort Worth, Texas

WHY WE LOVE HIM: He was a former professional boxer. He donated his $100,000 award for the Pritzker Architecture Prize to the orphans of the devastating 1995 earthquake in Kobe, Japan.

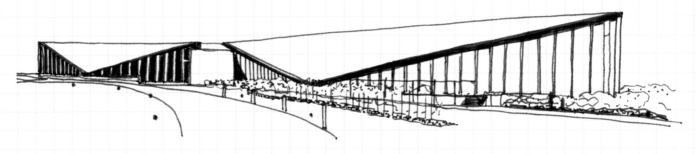

Above and Below: Modern Art Museum

HOLIDAY

SUGGESTED COOKIE:

S'mores (page 209)

Plain Custard Base (page 28) or Eggless Base (page 30), with 1 teaspoon freshly grated nutmeg added to cream mixture

¼ cup dark rum (such as Appleton Estate) or brandy

SPIKED EGGNOG ICE CREAM

MAKES ABOUT: 1½ quarts | **ACTIVE TIME:** 15 to 20 minutes

This is what Christmas really tastes like: a cup of Grandma's eggnog surreptitiously spiked with an illicit shot of brandy! Freshly grated nutmeg brings zip to the cream (ground nutmeg has much less impact).

1 Process base in an ice cream maker according to manufacturer's instructions. Add rum or brandy during last 2 minutes of churning.

2 Scrape into an airtight storage container. Freeze for a minimum of 2 hours before serving.

SWEET POTATO MARSHIE ICE CREAM

MAKES ABOUT: 1½ quarts | **ACTIVE TIME:** 15 to 20 minutes

We always thought our favorite Thanksgiving side dish should be a dessert. The best way to amp up the sweetness? Our secret ingredient: Marshie Fluff, instead of the usual mini marshmallows. The fluff lightens the texture, while bringing out the natural sugar and earthy qualities of the sweet potato.

1 Mix sweet potato into base with an immersion blender or a hand mixer until smooth.

2 Process in an ice cream maker according to manufacturer's instructions.

3 Transfer to a bowl and fold in Marshie Fluff.

4 Scrape into an airtight storage container. Freeze for a minimum of 2 hours before serving.

SUGGESTED COOKIES:

Snickerdoodle (page 194) or Maple Flapjack (page 200)

½ cup canned sweet potato puree (All-Natural Whole Foods Organic is good)

Plain Custard Base (page 28) or Eggless Base (page 30), made with brown sugar instead of white

¼ cup Marshie Fluff (Alternate Preparation, page 226) or store-bought

SUGGESTED COOKIE:

Snickerdoodle (page 194)

½ cup plus ⅔ cup granulated sugar

2 tablespoons cornstarch

2 cups fresh or frozen blueberries (Earthbound Farm and Safeway Organic are good frozen brands)

Juice of 1 lemon (about ¼ cup)

Pinch kosher salt

2 cups sifted all-purpose flour (sift before measuring)

1 stick (8 tablespoons) butter, melted

Plain Custard Base (page 28) or Eggless Base (page 30)

BLUEBERRY COBBLER ICE CREAM

MAKES ABOUT: 1½ quarts | **ACTIVE TIME:** 80 to 90 minutes

There are few better ways to cool off than with this ice cream. The recipe was inspired by Natasha's summers on Martha's Vineyard. Her family would wait all year for the two weeks in August when the blueberries were ripe and they could eat blueberry cobbler every night. Lemon turns up the berry volume, while the buttery cobbler crunch in the ice cream adds comfort. Best enjoyed while watching fireworks on the Fourth of July.

1   Preheat oven to 325 degrees. Lightly butter a 9-by-6-by-2-inch loaf pan or other baking pan.

2   Mix ½ cup sugar with cornstarch in a small bowl. Toss with berries to coat evenly. Add lemon juice and salt. Spoon into prepared pan. Set aside.

3   In a stand mixer or in a bowl with a whisk, mix flour and remaining ⅔ cup sugar. Drizzle with melted butter, stirring, to make a crumble topping. Cover blueberry mixture with topping.

4   Bake until bubbly and topping is golden brown, 45 to 50 minutes.

5   Let cool at room temperature, then refrigerate until cold, about 1 hour.

6   Process base in an ice cream maker according to manufacturer's instructions.

7   Transfer to a bowl. With a wooden spoon, break up blueberry crumble, then fold into ice cream.

8   Scrape into an airtight storage container. Freeze for a minimum of 2 hours before serving.

PUMPKIN PIE ICE CREAM

MAKES ABOUT: 1½ quarts | **ACTIVE TIME:** 30 to 35 minutes

We love to turn pies into ice cream. This one is great for Thanksgiving. Pumpkin pie spice, that familiar combo of nutmeg, allspice, cinnamon, and ginger, brings out the best in the squash, while our graham cracker "crust" makes it taste like a scoop of Thanksgiving.

1 Bring cream mixture in base to a boil. Stir in pumpkin pie spice while it is still hot. Proceed with base as directed.

2 Preheat oven to 325 degrees. Butter a baking sheet or line it with parchment paper.

3 In a small bowl, mix together graham cracker crumbs, sugar, and butter. Crumble mixture onto prepared baking sheet and toast in oven for 5 to 7 minutes, until gently browned. Let cool.

4 Mix pumpkin puree into base with an immersion blender or a hand mixer.

5 Process in an ice cream maker according to manufacturer's instructions.

6 Transfer to a bowl. Fold graham cracker crumbs into ice cream.

7 Scrape into an airtight storage container. Freeze for a minimum of 2 hours before serving.

SUGGESTED COOKIE:

Cinnamon Toast Crunch (page 197)

Plain Custard Base (page 28), prepared up to boiling step

2 teaspoons pumpkin pie spice

1 cup graham cracker crumbs (from 12 to 14 crackers)

¼ cup granulated sugar

3 tablespoons butter, melted

1 cup canned pumpkin puree (such as Libby's; do not use pumpkin pie mix)

TIP:

Make your own pumpkin pie spice by blending 1 teaspoon each of allspice, cinnamon, ginger, and nutmeg.

SUGGESTED COOKIE:

Double Chocolate Peppermint
(page 193)

Chocolate Custard Base (page 29)

4 large candy canes, broken into
pieces, or 12 Brach's Star Brites
candies, crushed

TIP:

To break up candy canes, place them
in a zip-top bag and bash them with a
rolling pin.

CHOCOLATE PEPPERMINT ICE CREAM

MAKES ABOUT: 1½ quarts | **ACTIVE TIME:** 15 to 20 minutes

Crunchy, bracing peppermint makes the chocolate base
dance in this seasonal favorite.

1 Process base in an ice cream maker according to manufacturer's
instructions.

2 Transfer to a bowl and fold in candy pieces.

3 Scrape into an airtight storage container. Freeze for a minimum of
2 hours before serving.

GELATOS & GELATO SANDWICHES

Our gelato flavors have all the signature power of Coolhaus ice cream, but with a stickier, almost chewier, texture than our ice cream.

NOTE: "Active times" do not include the making of the bases.

4 cups whole milk

1½ cups granulated sugar

8 large egg yolks

GELATO BASE

MAKES ABOUT: 1½ quarts | **ACTIVE TIME:** 10 to 15 minutes

Use the freshest eggs available for best results. If possible, refrigerate the base for a full 24 hours—the longer it's chilled, the better it is. We like to refrigerate our bases in plastic or stainless-steel pitchers with airtight lids for easy pouring into the ice cream maker after chilling.

1 In a 4-quart saucepan, combine milk and half of sugar. Set over high heat, and cook, stirring occasionally, until mixture comes to a boil, about 5 minutes.

2 Meanwhile, in a medium bowl, whisk yolks and remaining sugar until smooth, heavy, and pale yellow, about 30 seconds.

3 When cream mixture just comes to a boil, whisk, remove from heat, and, in a slow stream, pour half of cream mixture over yolk-sugar mixture, whisking constantly until blended.

4 Return pan to stovetop over low heat. Whisking constantly, stream yolk-cream mixture back into pan.

5 With a wooden spoon, continue stirring until mixture registers 165 to 180 degrees on an instant-read thermometer, about 2 minutes. Do not heat above 180 degrees, or eggs in base will scramble. Mixture should be slightly thickened and coat back of spoon, with steam rising, but not boiling. (If you blow on the back the of spoon and the mixture ripples, you've got the right consistency.)

6 Pour into a clean airtight container and refrigerate for 12 to 24 hours before using.

7 Use base within 3 to 5 days.

STRAWBERRY JALAPEÑO GELATO

MAKES ABOUT: 1½ quarts | **ACTIVE TIME:** 20 to 25 minutes

Oh, what this does to your tongue! Fruit and spice make everything nice. The sharp heat and cool cream blend to get the palate to stand at attention.

1   In a blender or food processor, puree strawberries, sugar, and lemon juice. Strain through a fine-mesh sieve into Gelato Base. Mix well.

2   Process in an ice cream maker according to manufacturer's instructions.

3   Transfer to a bowl and fold in diced jalapeño.

4   Scrape into an airtight storage container. Freeze for a minimum of 2 hours before serving.

SUGGESTED COOKIE:

Snickerdoodle (page 194)

12 to 14 strawberries, hulled

1 tablespoon granulated sugar

Juice of ½ lemon

Gelato Base (page 152)

½ jalapeño chile, seeded and finely diced

BLOOD ORANGE & CRANBERRY GELATO

MAKES ABOUT: 1½ quarts | **ACTIVE TIME:** 20 to 25 minutes

Tart, chewy dried cranberries balance this aromatic and citrusy gelato. It's bright and fruity, and we love the ruby-red color. A dash of fresh blood orange zest brings out all the flavor.

1 Prepare Gelato Base, adding half of orange zest to milk mixture before heating. Proceed as directed.

2 Mix blood orange juice into chilled base.

3 Process in an ice cream maker according to manufacturer's instructions.

4 Transfer to a bowl and fold in dried cranberries. Stir in remaining orange zest.

5 Scrape into an airtight storage container. Freeze for a minimum of 2 hours before serving.

SUGGESTED COOKIES:

Vegan Carrot Cake (page 212) or Double Chocolate (page 188)

Gelato Base (page 152)

Zest of 4 blood oranges, grated on a Microplane

1 cup blood orange juice (from 4 oranges)

½ cup dried cranberries

SUGGESTED COOKIE:

Vegan Ginger Molasses (page 217)

COOLHAUS SANDWICH CREATION:

Richard Meyer Lemon: Vegan Ginger Molasses Cookies + Meyer Lemon Gelato (see Building the Perfect Sandwich, page 25)

Gelato Base (page 152)

Zest of 3 Meyer lemons, grated on a Microplane

Juice of 2 Meyer lemons (about ½ cup)

MEYER LEMON GELATO

MAKES ABOUT: 1½ quarts | **ACTIVE TIME:** 20 to 25 minutes

A hybrid of sweet orange and sour lemon, Meyers are intensely perfumed and less acidic than regular lemons. Their zests and juice have become popular for desserts because of their delicate and sweet floral notes.

1 Prepare Gelato Base as directed, adding zest of 2 Meyer lemons to milk mixture before heating. Proceed as directed.

2 Stir lemon juice into chilled base.

3 Process in an ice cream maker according to manufacturer's instructions.

4 Transfer to a bowl and fold in remaining lemon zest.

5 Scrape into an airtight storage container. Freeze for a minimum of 2 hours before serving.

WHO IS
RICHARD MEIER?

A Jersey boy, born in Newark, Richard Meier was one of five New York architects who were mentored by Philip Johnson and inspired by Le Corbusier. Meier was so proficient that at forty-nine, he became the youngest architect to receive the Pritzker Architecture Prize.

STYLE: Rationalist modernism, which is all about geometry

MAJOR WORKS: The Getty Center, Los Angeles; Jubilee Church, Rome; New Harmony's Atheneum, New Harmony, Indiana; City Tower, Prague

WHY WE LOVE HIM: He's a Cornell alum (like Freya). He's an avid scrapbooker and collagist (not like Freya). His daughter came to the truck and requested the Richard Meyer Lemon sandwich—but we had run out of the flavor!

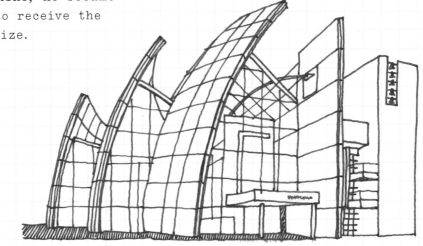

Jubilee Church

New Harmony's Atheneum

Strawberries &
Cream Gelato
(page 160)

SUGGESTED COOKIE:

Snickerdoodle (page 194)

COOLHAUS SANDWICH CREATION:

Frank Behry: Snickerdoodle Cookies + Strawberries & Cream Gelato (see Building the Perfect Sandwich, page 25)

12 to 14 strawberries

1 tablespoon granulated sugar

Juice of ½ lemon

Gelato Base (page 152)

STRAWBERRIES & CREAM GELATO

MAKES ABOUT: 1½ quarts | **ACTIVE TIME:** 20 to 25 minutes

You have a bowl of the freshest, ripest, juiciest strawberries. Sprinkle just a bit of sugar on top, and drown the berries in rich cream. Taste. Die and go to heaven. That's what this gelato is like.

1 In a blender or food processor, puree strawberries, sugar, and lemon juice. Strain through a fine-mesh sieve into Gelato Base. Mix well.

2 Process in an ice cream maker according to manufacturer's instructions.

3 Scrape into an airtight storage container. Freeze for a minimum of 2 hours before serving.

WHO IS
FRANK GEHRY?

Few works are as distinctive as this Canadian-born, Los Angeles–based architect's outside-of-the-box structures. Frank Gehry's undulating curves are unmistakable around the world, and he draws inspiration for his unorthodox "lines" from crumpled-up pieces of paper. "The most important architect of our age," as *Vanity Fair* christened him, has a penchant for titanium and an aversion to right angles.

Binoculars Building

STYLE: Deconstructivism

MAJOR WORKS: Guggenheim Museum Bilbao, Spain; Walt Disney Concert Hall, Los Angeles; Jay Pritzker Pavilion, Chicago; Binoculars Building, Venice Beach, California

WHY WE LOVE HIM: Frank Gehry came to our L.A. truck early on when we were selling by his office. He's short, and we have an awesome picture of him staring up at the truck, wondering, "What is this??" He didn't order his namesake, though—he is lactose-intolerant, so he had an Orange Julius Shulman (page 170).

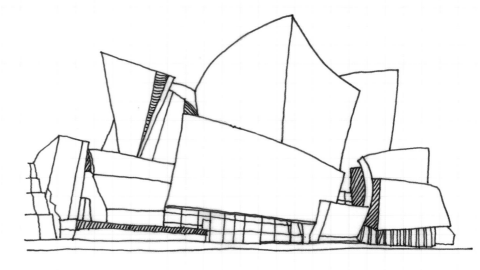

Walt Disney Concert Hall

SUGGESTED COOKIES:

Ginger Molasses (page 217) or
Snickerdoodle (page 194)

2 tablespoons Thai loose black tea (from an Asian market)

Gelato Base (page 152)

THAI ICED TEA GELATO

MAKES ABOUT: 1½ quarts | **ACTIVE TIME:** 20 to 25 minutes

The bright orange of this gelato is an ode to the Thai food scene that is so big in Los Angeles. The dairy base gives the rich sensation of condensed milk, and the black tea lends notes of star anise, tamarind, and cardamom.

1 Steep tea in hot milk–sugar mixture for 20 minutes, then strain through a fine-mesh sieve a few times until very few tea leaves are left.

2 Proceed with Gelato Base as directed.

3 Process chilled base in an ice cream maker according to manufacturer's instructions.

4 Scrape into an airtight storage container. Freeze for a minimum of 2 hours before serving.

SORBETS (VEGAN) & SORBET SANDWICHES

Sorbet is easy, refreshing, and delicious. For fruit sorbets, the key to ultimate deliciousness is using overripe, super-soft fruit. Those raspberries that are mushy and drippy? The strawberries that squash to the touch? The peaches that are so ripe they are incredibly aromatic? They are great for sorbet! A spritz of fresh lemon juice and a pinch of salt in the base bump up and brighten the fruit flavors. Bonus: All of our sorbets are vegan.

Some tips for sorbet making:

- You'll need to make and chill some simple syrup before preparing the sorbet.

- For best results, eat the sorbet within 2 weeks of making.

- A shot of tequila or rum (about 1 ounce) added to some of the following recipes brings life to the party!

- Active times do not include the making of the base.

2¼ cups granulated sugar

FOR BASE

2 cups Simple Syrup

Squeeze of fresh lemon juice

Pinch kosher salt

SORBET BASE

MAKES ABOUT: 2½ cups; 2 cups simple syrup | **ACTIVE TIME:** 10 minutes

The first step in making sorbet is simple syrup.

1. **Make Syrup:** in a 4-quart saucepan, combine sugar and 2 cups water. Bring to a boil over medium-high heat, stirring until sugar is dissolved.
2. Remove from heat and chill, about 30 minutes. (Syrup keeps, refrigerated in an airtight container, for up to 3 months.)
3. **Make Base:** Combine simple syrup, ½ cup water, lemon juice, and salt in a bowl. Stir well. (Base keeps, refrigerated in an airtight container, for up to 3 months.)

LEMON THYME SORBET

MAKES ABOUT: 1 quart | **ACTIVE TIME:** 15 to 20 minutes

Powerfully citrus and gently sour, this combination is invigorating. The herbaceous flavors evoke a scented breeze from the fields of southern France. It's the vegan version of Meyer Lemon Gelato (page 156).

1 In a 4-quart saucepan, combine sugar, thyme, and 2 cups water. Bring to a boil over medium heat and cook just until sugar dissolves. Let cool to room temperature, and then strain syrup through a fine-mesh sieve into a bowl.

2 Add lemon juice and ½ cup water to lemon thyme syrup.

3 Process in an ice cream maker according to manufacturer's instructions. Add lemon zest in last few seconds of churning, just before sorbet comes out of machine.

4 Scrape into an airtight storage container. Freeze for a minimum of 2 hours before serving.

SUGGESTED COOKIES:

Lemon Pine Nut Rosemary (page 198) or Vegan Ginger Molasses (page 217)

2 cups granulated sugar

10 sprigs fresh lemon thyme

2 cups fresh lemon juice (grate zest first)

Zest of 1 lemon, grated on a Microplane

BLACKBERRY GINGER SORBET

MAKES ABOUT: 1 quart | **ACTIVE TIME:** 15 to 20 minutes

SUGGESTED COOKIES:

Vegan Carrot Cake (page 212) or Vegan Ginger Molasses (page 217)

The perky heat from ginger brings a peppery edge to this sorbet. It also helps wake up the sour and sweet of the blackberries.

3 cups blackberries

¼ cup peeled and chopped fresh ginger

2 cups Sorbet Base (page 166)

1 In a blender or food processor, puree blackberries and ginger. Add Sorbet Base and blend to combine.

2 Process in an ice cream maker according to manufacturer's instructions.

3 Scrape into an airtight storage container. Freeze for a minimum of 2 hours before serving.

SUGGESTED COOKIES:

Vegan Ginger Molasses (page 217),
Double Chocolate (page 188), or
Snickerdoodle (page 194)

COOLHAUS SANDWICH
CREATION:

Orange Julius Shulman: Vegan Ginger
Molasses Cookies + Blood Orange Sorbet
(see Building the Perfect Sandwich,
page 25)

Sorbet Base (page 166)

2 cups fresh blood orange juice

BLOOD ORANGE SORBET

MAKES ABOUT: 1 quart | **ACTIVE TIME:** 15 to 20 minutes

A sweet, tart, and sour combo, with a deep ruby color, this sorbet is a great palate cleanser.

1   In a bowl, combine Sorbet Base, orange juice, and ½ cup water. Mix well.

2   Process in an ice cream maker according to manufacturer's instructions.

3   Scrape into an airtight storage container. Freeze for a minimum of 2 hours before serving.

WHO IS
JULIUS SHULMAN?

An American architectural photographer, Julius Shulman was known for documenting the work of architects such as Frank Lloyd Wright and Charles Eames and for furthering the popularity of the midcentury modern style in the 1940s to 1960s. Shulman's archive can be found at The Getty Center in Los Angeles.

STYLE: Midcentury modernist photography

MAJOR WORKS: Case Study House No. 22

WHY WE LOVE HIM: A documentarian is a welcome presence in a world where we are just as likely to knock down structures as to build them.

DARK CHOCOLATE SORBET

MAKES ABOUT: 1 quart | **ACTIVE TIME:** 20 to 25 minutes

Most people don't realize that dark chocolate is vegan—it contains no milk. This sorbet has the decadence of a chocolate ice cream with the added bonus of being dairy-free.

1 In a 4-quart saucepan, whisk together sugar, cocoa powder, espresso powder, salt, and 2½ cups water. Bring to a boil over medium-high heat, whisking constantly, until sugar dissolves.

2 Remove from heat and stir in chocolate until melted, then stir in vanilla extract.

3 Mix well with an immersion blender or a hand mixer until smooth.

4 Pour into a clean airtight container and refrigerate for 12 to 24 hours.

5 Process in an ice cream maker according to manufacturer's instructions. If the mixture has become too thick to pour into machine, whisk to thin it out first.

6 Scrape into an airtight storage container. Freeze for a minimum of 2 hours before serving.

SUGGESTED COOKIE:

Vegan Carrot Cake (page 212)

1 cup granulated sugar

1 cup unsweetened cocoa powder

1 tablespoon espresso powder

Pinch salt

1 cup finely chopped dark chocolate (at least 70% cacao)

½ teaspoon natural vanilla extract

SUGGESTED COOKIE:

Snickerdoodle (page 194)

COOLHAUS SANDWICH CREATION:

Gin & Arquitec-tonic-a: Snickerdoodle Cookies + Gin & Tonic Sorbet (see Building the Perfect Sandwich, page 25)

Sorbet Base (page 166)

1½ cups tonic water

¼ cup fresh lime juice (grate zest first)

1½ teaspoons juniper berry extract (see Tip)

¼ cup gin (we like Hendrick's)

Zest of 1 lime, grated on a Microplane

TIP:

You can get juniper berry extract from www.amazon.com.

GIN & TONIC SORBET

MAKES ABOUT: 1 quart | **ACTIVE TIME:** 15 to 20 minutes

The juniper flavor of the spirit takes wonderfully to the sorbet format: It's floral, effervescent, bitter, and dry.

1 Combine Sorbet Base, tonic water, lime juice, and juniper extract in a bowl.

2 Process in an ice cream maker according to manufacturer's instructions. Add gin during last 2 minutes of churning. Add zest and churn for a few seconds more.

3 Scrape into an airtight storage container. Freeze for a minimum of 2 hours before serving.

WHAT IS ARQUITECTONICA?

This Miami-based architecture, interior design, and landscape-planning firm is young and up-and-coming. It has designed buildings in forty countries around the world.

MAJOR WORKS: Four Seasons Dubai Hotel and Residences; High School for Construction Trades, Engineering and Architecture, New York City; Jorge Chávez International Airport, Peru

SUGGESTED COOKIES:

Vegan Ginger Molasses (page 217) or Gluten-Free Coconut Almond Chocolate Chip (page 214)

2 (20-ounce) cans lychees with juice

Sorbet Base (page 166)

¼ cup Hendrick's gin (or equal amount of vodka, if you prefer)

TIP:

Lychees are found in Asian markets and in the international foods aisles of large supermarkets.

LYCHEE MARTINI SORBET

MAKES ABOUT: 1 quart | **ACTIVE TIME:** 15 to 20 minutes

Delicately sweet lychee latches easily onto the rose hip and cucumber profile of Hendrick's gin. The result is a mellowly tropical eye-opener.

1 In a blender or food processor, puree lychees and their juice. Strain through a fine-mesh sieve into a bowl.

2 Add Sorbet Base and ½ cup water to lychee puree and stir to combine.

3 Process in an ice cream maker according to manufacturer's instructions. Add gin during last 2 minutes of churning.

4 Scrape into an airtight storage container. Freeze for a minimum of 2 hours before serving.

PEACH BELLINI SORBET

MAKES ABOUT: 1 quart | **ACTIVE TIME:** 15 to 20 minutes

White peaches have a gentler, more floral sweetness than their yellow counterparts. Their flavor pairs nicely with prosecco, which gives this sorbet a nice pop.

1. In a bowl, combine peach puree, Sorbet Base, and ½ cup water and mix well.

2. Process in an ice cream maker according to manufacturer's instructions. Add prosecco during last 2 minutes of churning.

3. Scrape into an airtight storage container. Freeze for a minimum of 2 hours before serving.

SUGGESTED COOKIES:

Snickerdoodle (page 194) or Vegan Ginger Molasses (page 217)

---

2 cups pureed peaches (from 4 white or yellow peeled peaches)

Sorbet Base (page 166)

1 cup prosecco

TIP:

To peel peaches, bring a saucepan of water to a boil. Transfer peaches to water with a slotted spoon, cook for 30 seconds, remove with the spoon, and plunge into a bowl of ice and water. The skins will slip off.

SUGGESTED COOKIE:

Vegan Ginger Molasses (page 217)

COOLHAUS SANDWICH CREATION:

Thom Mayne-go: Vegan Ginger Molasses Cookies + Mango Sorbet (see Building the Perfect Sandwich, page 25)

Sorbet Base (page 166)

2 cups pureed mango (from 4 cups chopped mango)

Juice of 1 lime

TIP:

You can order mango puree from www .perfectpuree.com.

MANGO SORBET

MAKES ABOUT: 1 quart | **ACTIVE TIME:** 15 to 20 minutes

Intensely sweet, slightly puckery, exotic, and luscious—this is our pick for a desert island sorbet.

1   In a bowl, combine Sorbet Base, mango puree, lime juice, and ½ cup water and mix well.

2   Process in an ice cream maker according to manufacturer's instructions.

3   Scrape into an airtight storage container. Freeze for a minimum of 2 hours before serving.

WHO IS
THOM MAYNE?

A founder of the Southern California Institute of Architecture (SCI-Arc), Mayne is a principal of Morphosis, a Santa Monica–based architectural firm. Morphosis' design mission is to enforce "a dynamic and evolving practice that responds to the shifting and advancing social, cultural, political, and technological conditions of modern life."

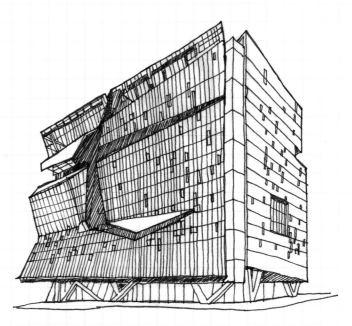

41 Cooper Square

STYLE: Countercultural shape-changing

MAJOR WORKS: Sun Tower, Seoul, Korea; San Francisco Federal Building, San Francisco; Caltrans District 7 Headquarters, Los Angeles; Perot Museum of Nature and Science, Dallas, Texas; 41 Cooper Square, New York City

WHY WE LOVE HIM: Mayne is a risk-taker who describes his style as "idiosyncratic." We appreciate that at Coolhaus.

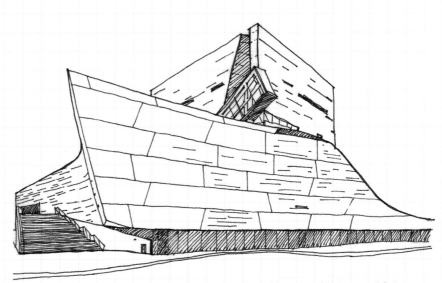

Perot Museum of Nature and Science

SUGGESTED COOKIES:

Snickerdoodle (page 194), Vegan Ginger Molasses (page 217), or Vegan Carrot Cake (page 212)

3 cups fresh or frozen strawberries (Earthbound Farm and Safeway Organic are good frozen brands)

4 sprigs fresh mint

Juice of 1 lime

Sorbet Base (page 166), made with packed light brown sugar

2 ounces (¼ cup) white rum

STRAWBERRY MOJITO SORBET

MAKES ABOUT: 1 quart | **ACTIVE TIME:** 15 to 20 minutes

Nothing wakes up strawberries like a nice hint of mint. White rum adds a syrupy and spirited beat.

1 In a blender or food processor, puree strawberries and mint. Strain through a fine-mesh sieve into a bowl. Discard any solids left in sieve.

2 Add lime juice, Sorbet Base, and ½ cup water to strawberry puree and mix well.

3 Process in an ice cream maker according to manufacturer's instructions. Add rum during last 2 minutes of churning.

4 Scrape into an airtight storage container. Freeze for a minimum of 2 hours before serving.

PEAR VANILLA SORBET

MAKES ABOUT: 1 quart | **ACTIVE TIME:** 40 to 60 minutes

We think of pears as introverted apples. And what better flavor to play up this wallflower fruit than vanilla? A little white wine adds some personality (we recommend using a nice Grüner Veltliner or Riesling). It's true that this sorbet takes a little more time than our other sorbets, but like a liquefied poached pear, it is well worth the extra effort.

1   In a bowl, combine Sorbet Base and pear puree and mix well.

2   Process in an ice cream maker according to manufacturer's instructions.

3   Scrape into an airtight storage container. Freeze for a minimum of 2 hours before serving.

SUGGESTED COOKIES:

Vegan Ginger Molasses (page 217) or Gluten-Free Coconut Almond Chocolate Chip (page 214)

Sorbet Base (page 166)

2 cups Pear Puree (recipe follows)

PEAR PUREE

1 (750-ml) bottle dry white wine

2 cups granulated sugar

1 vanilla bean, split, seeds scraped

Pinch kosher salt

8 Bosc or Bartlett pears, peeled, cored, and coarsely chopped

In a 4-quart saucepan, combine wine, sugar, vanilla bean seeds and pod, salt, and 3 cups water. Bring to a boil over medium-high heat.

Add pears and return mixture to a boil. Reduce heat to low and cook until pears are soft and tender, 20 to 30 minutes.

Remove and discard vanilla bean pod. Puree in a blender. Strain through a fine-mesh sieve into a bowl and let cool.

SUGGESTED COOKIES:

Snickerdoodle (page 194), Vegan Ginger Molasses (page 217), or Vegan Carrot Cake (page 212)

1 very ripe pineapple, peeled, cored, and chopped

6 tablespoons chopped fresh cilantro leaves

1 serrano chile, stemmed and seeded

Sorbet Base (page 166)

SPICY PINEAPPLE-CILANTRO-CHILE SORBET

MAKES ABOUT: 1 quart | **ACTIVE TIME:** 15 to 20 minutes

Reminiscent of a pineapple slushy, but with a sophisticated edge, this is a lighter spin on the zippy, fruity, herbal ice cream on page 58. Its flavor is more like a fiery and fruity Mexican salsa than a piña colada.

1 In a food processor or blender, puree pineapple, cilantro, and serrano. Transfer pineapple puree to a bowl and stir in Sorbet Base.

2 Process in an ice cream maker according to manufacturer's instructions.

3 Scrape into an airtight storage container. Freeze for a minimum of 2 hours before serving.

In the beginning, we were pretty bad at baking. We weren't great at keeping track of exactly what and how much of each ingredient we were putting into the cookie recipes. And when we say "we," we mean Natasha.

Freya would ask, "What did you do with this batch versus that batch?"

Natasha would answer, "I don't know. I just went on instinct." That's when Freya's head would explode.

Baking has rules. But Coolhaus cookies play by their own rules. So forget everything you learned from your home ec class or expert baker aunt and pay attention to the Coolhaus way.

Our basic method is to mix the wet ingredients, mix the dry ingredients, add them to the wet, fold in any inclusions, chill the dough, shape it, and bake. Not rocket science, but still a bit of a science.

THE COOLHAUS COOKIE CREDO

Cookies meant for ice cream sandwiches have their own distinct properties, necessary to effectively carry the ice cream. The perfect Coolhaus sandwich cookie is soft, chewy, and pliable; about 3 inches in diameter; wraps around the ice cream, stands up to it, and holds it in place while eating. To create our signature texture, we use a lot of brown sugar and melted butter, not much baking soda, and sometimes more egg yolks than whites. Also, we essentially create pastry flour at home by blending cake flour and all-purpose flour. All of these tweaks make for a chewier, flatter, ice cream–ready cookie.

NOTE: "Active times" do not include refrigerating the dough.

BAKING NOTES

Our recommended baking temperature is for **standard ovens.** If you are using a convection oven, set the temperature 25 to 50 degrees lower.

We like to bake on **parchment paper–lined** baking sheets for best results. If parchment paper is not available, however, you can use a Silpat liner or put the cookies directly on a buttered baking sheet.

Be sure to **cool the butter** before you add it to the wet ingredients. If it is too hot when added to the eggs, it will cook the eggs.

KNOW YOUR FLOURS

In some cookies, our **flour blend i**s the key to success. Know which flour you are purchasing! These are the four flours you'll need for our cookies:

All-purpose: basic, common white flour; a blend of high-gluten hard wheat and low-gluten soft wheat

Bread flour: strong, hard, high-gluten wheat flour

Cake flour: finely textured, starchy, soft flour

Gluten-free flour (such as almond flour): for gluten-free cookies

Our recipes use pastry flour or a blend of all-purpose flour and cake flour, which yields a moist, chewier cookie.

Always **sift flour** before measuring.

Always use **dry measuring cups** made for dry ingredients (as opposed to liquid/volume measuring cups).

When measuring flour, scoop the amount of flour you want with the dry measuring cup and **level it off** with the flat back of a knife.

Sifting the dry ingredients makes for better, more consistent cookies. The process breaks up lumps and evenly distributes the balance of dry ingredients throughout the cookie. Don't have a sifter? Don't worry—simply use a whisk to "fluff" up dry ingredients and eliminate lumps or use a fine-mesh sieve set over a bowl.

When measuring brown sugar, **pack it in**—the opposite process of measuring flour!

Chill the dough for at least 20 minutes before shaping it so it is easier to handle. Note that in general, most of our doughs are on the wet side.

Stand mixers work best for consistently mixing cookie dough, but hand mixers are fine.

To store leftover dough, roll it up into a roughly 3-inch log and wrap in plastic. When you are ready to use, cut it into ¼-inch-thick pucks, and bake.

Wrapped well, cookie dough can be kept in the refrigerator for up to 2 weeks or frozen for up to 3 months.

CLASSIC

CHOCOLATE CHIP COOKIES

MAKES: 20 to 24 cookies | **ACTIVE TIME:** 20 to 25 minutes

We use light brown and dark brown sugar to give our chocolate chip cookies a caramel-y chewiness. This is a classic flavor, with our signature sturdy, yet pliant, texture.

1 **Mix wets:** Place butter in a saucepan and set over low heat until just half is melted. Cool for 5 minutes.

2 Pour cooled butter into a large bowl. Add both sugars and whisk to combine. Whisk in egg and yolk, one at a time, then whisk in vanilla. Set aside.

3 **Mix dries:** In a medium bowl, whisk together flour, salt, and baking soda.

4 Add dries, one third at a time, to wets, mixing with a rubber spatula or wooden spoon to combine. Fold in chocolate chips until evenly distributed.

5 Wrap bowl with plastic wrap and refrigerate for at least 20 minutes.

6 Preheat oven to 325 degrees, with racks in lower and upper thirds of oven. Line two half-sheet baking pans with parchment paper.

7 Form dough into balls about the size of whole walnuts and place 2 inches apart on prepared baking sheets.

8 Bake for 10 to 12 minutes, or until edges are light brown and centers are still wet—don't overbake.

9 Immediately transfer cookies to a cooling rack. Let cool for 1 hour before serving.

- 2 sticks (16 tablespoons) unsalted butter
- 1 cup packed light brown sugar
- 1 cup packed dark brown sugar
- 1 large egg plus 1 large egg yolk
- 1½ teaspoons natural vanilla extract
- 2½ cups sifted pastry flour, or 2 cups sifted all-purpose flour plus ½ cup sifted cake flour (sift before measuring)
- ½ teaspoon kosher salt
- ½ teaspoon baking soda
- 1 cup semisweet chocolate chips (we like Guittard, TCHO, Mast Brothers, or Ghirardelli)

2 sticks (16 tablespoons) unsalted butter

2 cups packed light brown sugar

1 large egg plus 1 large egg yolk

1 teaspoon natural vanilla extract

2 cups sifted pastry flour, or 1¾ cups sifted all-purpose flour plus ¼ cup sifted cake flour (sift before measuring)

¾ cup unsweetened cocoa powder

½ teaspoon kosher salt

½ teaspoon baking soda

1 cup semisweet chocolate chips (we like Guittard or Ghirardelli)

DOUBLE CHOCOLATE COOKIES

MAKES: 20 to 24 cookies | **ACTIVE TIME:** 20 to 25 minutes

Rich, gooey, chewy, and sublime—these dark chocolate cookies combine the highest-quality dark chocolate chunks with cocoa powder. As in all of our cookies, there's a generous lacing of butter.

1 **Mix wets:** Place butter in a saucepan and set over low heat until just half is melted. Cool for 5 minutes.

2 Pour cooled butter into a large bowl. Add sugar and whisk to combine. Whisk in egg and yolk, one at a time, then whisk in vanilla. Set aside.

3 **Mix dries:** In a medium bowl, whisk together flour, cocoa powder, salt, and baking soda.

4 Add dries, one third at a time, to wets, mixing with a rubber spatula or wooden spoon to combine. Fold in chocolate chips until evenly distributed.

5 Wrap bowl with plastic wrap and refrigerate for at least 20 minutes.

6 Preheat oven to 325 degrees, with racks in lower and upper thirds of oven. Line two half-sheet baking pans with parchment paper.

7 Form dough into balls about the size of whole walnuts and place 2 inches apart on prepared baking sheets.

8 Bake for 10 to 12 minutes, or until edges are light brown and centers are still wet—don't overbake.

9 Immediately transfer cookies to a cooling rack. Let cool for 1 hour before serving.

Ingredients

- 2 sticks (16 tablespoons) unsalted butter
- 2 cups packed light brown sugar
- 1 large egg plus 1 large egg yolk
- 1 teaspoon natural vanilla extract
- 2 cups sifted pastry flour, or 1¾ cups sifted all-purpose flour plus ¼ cup sifted cake flour (sift before measuring)
- ¾ cup unsweetened cocoa powder
- ½ teaspoon kosher salt
- ½ teaspoon baking soda
- 1 cup semisweet chocolate chips (we like Guittard or Ghirardelli)
- 2 tablespoons Maldon sea salt

DOUBLE CHOCOLATE SEA SALT COOKIES

MAKES: 20 to 24 cookies | **ACTIVE TIME:** 20 to 25 minutes

This cookie has everything its simpler counterpart does, with a brightening edge of sea salt.

1 **Mix wets:** Place butter in a saucepan and set over low heat until just half is melted. Cool for 5 minutes.

2 Pour cooled butter into a large bowl. Add sugar and whisk to combine. Whisk in egg and yolk, one at a time, then whisk in vanilla. Set aside.

3 **Mix dries:** In a medium bowl, whisk together flour, cocoa powder, kosher salt, and baking soda.

4 Add dries, one third at a time, to wets, mixing with a rubber spatula or wooden spoon to combine. Fold in chocolate chips until evenly distributed.

5 Wrap bowl with plastic wrap and refrigerate for at least 20 minutes.

6 Preheat oven to 325 degrees, with racks in lower and upper thirds of oven. Line two half-sheet baking pans with parchment paper.

7 Form dough into balls about the size of whole walnuts and place 2 inches apart on prepared baking sheets.

8 Top each cookie with a few flakes of sea salt and push down gently.

9 Bake for 10 to 12 minutes, or until edges are light brown and centers are still wet—don't overbake.

10 Immediately transfer cookies to a cooling rack. Let cool for 1 hour before serving.

OATMEAL RAISIN COOKIES

MAKES: 20 to 24 cookies | **ACTIVE TIME:** 20 to 25 minutes

Nothing fancy here—just everything you would expect from a wholesome oatmeal cookie: chewy, sweet raisins, a generous spike of cinnamon, and dense rolled oats.

1. **Mix wets:** Place butter in a saucepan and set over low heat until just half is melted. Cool for 5 minutes.

2. Pour cooled butter into a large bowl. Add sugar and whisk to combine. Whisk in egg and yolk, one at a time, then whisk in vanilla. Set aside.

3. **Mix dries:** In a medium bowl, whisk together flour, salt, baking soda, and cinnamon.

4. Add dries, one third at a time, to wets, mixing with a rubber spatula or wooden spoon to combine. Mix in oats and raisins.

5. Wrap bowl with plastic wrap and refrigerate for at least 20 minutes.

6. Preheat oven to 325 degrees, with racks in lower and upper thirds of oven. Line two half-sheet baking pans with parchment paper.

7. Form dough into balls about the size of whole walnuts and place 2 inches apart on prepared baking sheets.

8. Bake for 12 to 14 minutes, or until edges are light brown and centers are still wet—don't overbake.

9. Immediately transfer cookies to a cooling rack. Cool for 1 hour before serving.

2 sticks (16 tablespoons) unsalted butter

2 cups packed light brown sugar

1 large egg plus 1 large egg yolk

1 teaspoon natural vanilla extract

2 cups sifted pastry flour, or 1¾ cups sifted all-purpose flour plus ¼ cup sifted cake flour (sift before measuring)

½ teaspoon kosher salt

½ teaspoon baking soda

½ teaspoon ground cinnamon

2½ cups old-fashioned rolled oats

1 cup raisins

DOUBLE CHOCOLATE PEPPERMINT COOKIES

MAKES: 18 cookies | **ACTIVE TIME:** 20 to 25 minutes

This combination of double dark chocolate cookies topped with peppermint patty candies is like having a minty arctic breeze blow into your mouth with each bite. These are perfect for the holidays!

1. **Mix wets:** Place butter in a saucepan and set over low heat until just half is melted. Cool for 5 minutes.

2. Pour cooled butter into a large bowl. Add sugar and whisk to combine. Whisk in egg and yolk, one at a time, then whisk in vanilla. Set aside.

3. **Mix dries:** In a medium bowl, whisk together flour, cocoa powder, salt, and baking soda.

4. Add dries, one third at a time, to wets, mixing with a rubber spatula or wooden spoon to combine. Fold in chocolate chips until evenly distributed.

5. Wrap bowl with plastic wrap and refrigerate for at least 20 minutes.

6. Preheat oven to 325 degrees, with racks in lower and upper thirds of oven. Line two half-sheet baking pans with parchment paper.

7. Form dough into 18 balls and place 2 inches apart on prepared baking sheets. Top each cookie with 1 peppermint patty. Push down gently.

8. Bake for 10 to 12 minutes, or until edges have set, centers are still wet, and middle of cookies stick to your finger; don't overbake.

9. Immediately transfer cookies to a cooling rack. Let cool for 1 hour before serving.

- 2 sticks (16 tablespoons) unsalted butter
- 2 cups packed light brown sugar
- 1 large egg plus 1 large egg yolk
- 1 teaspoon natural vanilla extract
- 2 cups sifted pastry flour or 1¾ cups sifted all-purpose flour plus ¼ cup sifted cake flour (sift before measuring)
- ¾ cup unsweetened cocoa powder
- ½ teaspoon kosher salt
- ½ teaspoon baking soda
- 1 cup semisweet chocolate chips (we like Guittard or Ghirardelli)
- 18 mini York peppermint patties

SNICKERDOODLE COOKIES

MAKES: 20 to 24 cookies | **ACTIVE TIME:** 20 to 25 minutes

- 2 sticks (16 tablespoons) unsalted butter

- 1½ cups plus 3 tablespoons granulated sugar

- 3 large eggs

- 1 teaspoon natural vanilla extract

- 1 tablespoon ground cinnamon

- 2½ cups sifted all-purpose flour (sift before measuring)

- ¼ teaspoon kosher salt

- 1 teaspoon cream of tartar

- ¼ teaspoon baking soda

We love the word *snickerdoodle*—it's so much more fun to say than "sugar cookie." Cinnamon makes this perky. The butter and sugar come through here, with a dash of salt to wake up the simple pleasure.

1 **Mix wets:** Place butter in a saucepan and set over low heat until just half is melted. Cool for 5 minutes.

2 Pour cooled butter into a large bowl. Add 1½ cups of sugar and whisk to combine. Whisk in eggs, one at a time, then whisk in vanilla. Whisk until mixture has consistency of wet sand. Set aside.

3 **Mix dries:** In a small bowl, whisk cinnamon and remaining 3 tablespoons sugar. Set aside.

4 In a medium bowl, whisk together flour, salt, cream of tartar, and baking soda.

5 Add dries, one third at a time, to wets, mixing with a rubber spatula or wooden spoon to combine.

6 Wrap bowl with plastic wrap and refrigerate for at least 20 minutes.

7 Preheat oven to 325 degrees, with racks in lower and upper thirds. Line two half-sheet baking pans with parchment paper.

8 Form dough into balls about the size of whole walnuts and roll them in reserved cinnamon-sugar mixture. Set cookie balls 2 inches apart on prepared baking sheets.

9 Bake for 12 to 14 minutes, or until edges are light brown and centers are still wet; don't overbake.

10 Immediately transfer cookies to a cooling rack. Let cool for 1 hour before serving.

CREATIVE

CINNAMON TOAST CRUNCH COOKIES

MAKES: 20 to 24 cookies | **ACTIVE TIME:** 20 to 25 minutes

We combine the sensation of crunchy French toast and the famous cereal in these crispy cookies.

1 **Mix wets:** Place butter in a saucepan and set over low heat until just half is melted. Cool for 5 minutes.

2 Pour cooled butter into a large bowl. Add brown sugar and 1½ cups of granulated sugar and whisk to combine. Whisk in egg and yolk, one at a time, then whisk in vanilla. Set aside.

3 **Mix dries:** In a small bowl, whisk together remaining 3 tablespoons granulated sugar and 1 tablespoon of cinnamon. Set aside.

4 In a medium bowl, whisk together remaining 1 teaspoon cinnamon, salt, baking soda, and flour.

5 Add dries, one third at a time, to wets, mixing with a rubber spatula or wooden spoon to combine. Add crushed cereal, mixing until evenly distributed. (Mixing will further crush cereal—be careful not to overmix and overcrush it.)

6 Wrap bowl with plastic wrap and refrigerate for at least 20 minutes.

7 Preheat oven to 325 degrees, with racks in upper and lower thirds of oven. Line two half-sheet baking pans with parchment paper.

8 Form dough into balls about the size of whole walnuts and roll in cinnamon-sugar mixture. Place cookies 2 inches apart on prepared baking sheets. Sprinkle each cookie with some uncrushed cereal.

9 Bake for 10 to 12 minutes, or until edges are light brown and centers are still wet—don't overbake.

10 Immediately transfer cookies to a cooling rack. Let cool for 1 hour before serving.

- 2 sticks (16 tablespoons) unsalted butter
- ¼ cup packed dark brown sugar
- 1½ cups plus 3 tablespoons granulated sugar
- 1 large egg plus 1 large egg yolk
- 1½ teaspoons natural vanilla extract
- 1 teaspoon plus 1 tablespoon ground cinnamon
- ½ teaspoon kosher salt
- ¼ teaspoon baking soda
- 2½ cups sifted pastry flour, or 2 cups sifted all-purpose flour plus ½ cup sifted cake flour (sift before measuring)
- 1 cup crushed Cinnamon Toast Crunch cereal, plus 1 handful uncrushed for sprinkling

½ cup pine nuts

2 sticks (16 tablespoons) unsalted butter

¾ cup packed light brown sugar

¾ cup granulated sugar

1 large egg plus 1 large egg yolk

1 teaspoon olive oil

2¾ cups sifted pastry flour, or 2 cups sifted all-purpose flour plus ¾ cup sifted cake flour (sift before measuring)

½ teaspoon kosher salt

½ teaspoon baking soda

2 teaspoons grated lemon zest, grated on a Microplane

2 tablespoons finely chopped fresh rosemary

LEMON PINE NUT ROSEMARY COOKIES

MAKES: 20 to 24 cookies | **ACTIVE TIME:** 20 to 25 minutes

These are sophisticated cookies, the kind you might be offered at a swanky high tea at Harrods in London. We love the pliancy of pine nuts, the herbal edge of rosemary, and the vitality that a tweak of lemon adds to these great snacks.

1 Preheat oven to 325 degrees. Spread pine nuts on a baking sheet and toast in oven for 5 to 7 minutes, until gently toasted, not browned. Set aside. Turn off oven.

2 **Mix wets:** Place butter in a saucepan and set over low heat until just half is melted. Cool for 5 minutes.

3 Pour cooled butter into a large bowl. Add both sugars and whisk to combine. Whisk in egg and yolk, one at a time, then whisk in olive oil. Set aside.

4 **Mix dries:** In a medium bowl, whisk together flour, salt, and baking soda.

5 Add dries, one third at a time, to wets, mixing with a rubber spatula or wooden spoon to combine. Fold in toasted pine nuts and lemon zest until evenly distributed.

6 Wrap bowl with plastic wrap and refrigerate for at least 20 minutes.

7 Preheat oven to 325 degrees, with racks in upper and lower thirds. Line two half-sheet baking pans with parchment paper.

8 Form dough into balls about the size of whole walnuts and place 2 inches apart on prepared baking sheets.

9 Press a generous pinch of rosemary on top of each cookie.

10 Bake for 10 to 12 minutes, or until edges are light brown and centers are still wet—don't overbake.

11 Immediately transfer cookies to a cooling rack. Let cool for 1 hour before serving.

2 sticks (16 tablespoons) unsalted butter

1 cup packed dark brown sugar

1 cup maple sugar (see headnote)

1 large egg plus 1 large egg yolk

1 teaspoon maple extract

2½ cups sifted pastry flour, or 2 cups sifted all-purpose flour plus ½ cup sifted cake flour (sift before measuring)

½ teaspoon salt

½ teaspoon baking soda

MAPLE FLAPJACK COOKIES

MAKES: 20 to 24 cookies **│ ACTIVE TIME:** 20 to 25 minutes

Flapjacks are a natural with our ice creams, especially because of their maple syrup boost. These are great with "breakfast" ice creams like Brown Butter Candied Bacon (page 126), Fried Chicken & Waffle (page 120), Whiskey Lucky Charms (page 83), and Froot Loops & Milk (page 50).

Brown sugar can be substituted for the maple sugar for a similar effect.

1 **Mix wets:** Place butter in a saucepan and set over low heat until just half is melted. Cool for 5 minutes.

2 Pour cooled butter into a large bowl. Add both sugars and whisk to combine. Whisk in egg and yolk, one at a time, then whisk in maple extract. Set aside.

3 **Mix dries:** In a medium bowl, whisk together flour, salt, and baking soda.

4 Add dries, one third at a time, to wets, mixing with a rubber spatula or wooden spoon to combine. Dough will be goopy.

5 Wrap bowl with plastic wrap and refrigerate for at least 20 minutes.

6 Preheat oven to 325 degrees, with racks in upper and lower thirds. Line two half-sheet baking pans with parchment paper.

7 Form dough into balls about the size of whole walnuts and place 2 inches apart on prepared baking sheets.

8 Bake for 12 to 14 minutes, or until edges are light brown and centers are still wet—don't overbake.

9 Immediately transfer cookies to a cooling rack. Let cool for 1 hour before serving.

PUMPKIN PIE COOKIES

MAKES: 20 to 24 cookies | **ACTIVE TIME:** 20 to 25 minutes

We love the cakey texture of these cookies, which make a perfect vehicle for the holiday-evoking spice blend of allspice, ginger, cinnamon, and nutmeg.

1 **Mix wets:** Place butter in a saucepan and set over low heat until just half is melted. Cool for 5 minutes.

2 Pour cooled butter into a large bowl. Add brown sugar and whisk to combine. Stir in pumpkin puree until blended. Whisk in egg, then whisk in vanilla. Set aside.

3 **Mix dries:** In a medium bowl, whisk together flour, pumpkin pie spice, salt, and baking soda.

4 Add dries, one third at a time, to wets, mixing with a rubber spatula or wooden spoon to combine.

5 Wrap bowl with plastic wrap and refrigerate for at least 20 minutes.

6 Preheat oven to 325 degrees, with racks in upper and lower thirds. Line two half-sheet baking pans with parchment paper.

7 Form dough into balls about the size of whole walnuts and place 2 inches apart on prepared baking sheets.

8 Bake for 10 to 12 minutes, or until edges are light brown and centers are still wet—don't overbake.

9 Immediately transfer cookies to a cooling rack. Let cool for 1 hour before serving.

---

2 sticks (16 tablespoons) unsalted butter

2 cups packed light brown sugar

½ cup canned pumpkin puree (such as Libby's; do not use pumpkin pie mix)

1 large egg

1½ teaspoons natural vanilla extract

2½ cups sifted pastry flour, or 2 cups sifted all-purpose flour plus ½ cup sifted cake flour (sift before measuring)

1 tablespoon pumpkin pie spice

½ teaspoon kosher salt

¼ teaspoon baking soda

2 sticks (16 tablespoons) unsalted butter

1 cup packed light brown sugar

1 cup packed dark brown sugar

1 large egg plus 1 large egg yolk

1¼ teaspoons natural vanilla extract

2½ cups sifted pastry flour, or 2 cups sifted all-purpose flour plus ½ cup sifted cake flour (sift before measuring)

½ teaspoon kosher salt

½ teaspoon baking soda

1 cup semisweet chocolate chips (we like Guittard or Ghirardelli)

1 cup crushed salted pretzels

PRETZEL CHOCOLATE CHUNK COOKIES

MAKES: 20 to 24 cookies | **ACTIVE TIME:** 20 to 25 minutes

Here, in cookie form, is the ultimate trail mix: salty pretzels and semisweet chocolate chips. It's the perfect backpack stash for hiking cookie emergencies.

1 **Mix wets:** Place butter in a saucepan and set over low heat until just half is melted. Cool for 5 minutes.

2 Pour cooled butter into a large bowl. Add both sugars and whisk to combine. Whisk in egg and egg yolk, one at a time, then whisk in vanilla.

3 **Mix dries:** In a medium bowl, whisk together flour, salt, and baking soda.

4 Add dries, one third at a time, to wets, mixing with a rubber spatula or wooden spoon to combine. Fold in chocolate chips and pretzels until evenly distributed.

5 Wrap bowl with plastic wrap and refrigerate for at least 20 minutes.

6 Preheat oven to 325 degrees, with racks in upper and lower thirds. Line two half-sheet baking pans with parchment paper.

7 Form dough into balls about the size of whole walnuts and place 2 inches apart on prepared baking sheets.

8 Bake for 10 to 12 minutes, or until edges are light brown and centers are still wet—don't overbake.

9 Immediately transfer cookies to a cooling rack. Let cool for 1 hour before serving.

FOR COOKIES

2 sticks (16 tablespoons) unsalted butter

1 cup packed light brown sugar

1 cup packed dark brown sugar

1 large egg plus 1 large egg yolk

1 teaspoon natural vanilla extract

2½ cups sifted pastry flour, or 2 cups sifted all-purpose flour plus ½ cup sifted cake flour (sift before measuring)

1 tablespoon unsweetened cocoa powder

½ teaspoon salt

½ teaspoon baking soda

1 tablespoon red food coloring (such as McCormick)

FOR ICING

4 ounces cream cheese, at room temperature

1 stick (8 tablespoons) unsalted butter, at room temperature

2 cups sifted powdered sugar (sift before measuring)

½ teaspoon natural vanilla extract

RED VELVET COOKIES

MAKES: 20 to 24 cookies | **ACTIVE TIME:** 20 to 25 minutes

We heart everything about red velvet. The cheerful red color. The deep cocoa flavor. It's a sugary, buttery, chocolaty cookie that makes the perfect Valentine's Day treat.

MAKE COOKIES

1 **Mix wets:** Place butter in a saucepan and set over low heat until just half is melted. Cool for 5 minutes.

2 Pour cooled butter into a large bowl. Add both sugars and whisk to combine. Whisk in egg and yolk, one at a time, and then whisk in vanilla. Set aside.

3 **Mix dries:** In a medium bowl, whisk together flour, cocoa powder, salt, and baking soda.

4 Add dries, one third at a time, to wets, mixing with a rubber spatula or wooden spoon to combine. Add food coloring. Mix until color is uniform.

5 Wrap bowl with plastic wrap and refrigerate for at least 20 minutes.

6 Preheat oven to 325 degrees, with racks in upper and lower thirds. Line two half-sheet baking pans with parchment paper.

7 Form dough into balls about the size of whole walnuts and place 2 inches apart on prepared baking sheets.

8 Bake for 10 to 12 minutes, or until edges are light brown and centers are still wet—don't overbake.

9 Immediately transfer cookies to a cooling rack. Let cool for 1 hour before icing.

MEANWHILE, MAKE ICING

10 Using a stand or hand mixer on medium-high, beat cream cheese and butter together until smooth and fluffy, 2 to 3 minutes. Add powdered sugar, starting on low speed, then working up to high speed. Add vanilla.

11 Using a pastry bag or a zip-top bag with one corner snipped, ice cooled cookies in the pattern of your liking and serve.

2 cups packed light brown sugar

½ cup crunchy peanut butter (we like Whole Foods or Justin's)

1 large egg plus 1 large egg yolk

1 teaspoon natural vanilla extract

3 tablespoons granulated sugar

1 tablespoon ground cinnamon

2½ cups sifted pastry flour, or 2 cups sifted all-purpose flour plus ½ cup sifted cake flour (sift before measuring)

½ teaspoon kosher salt

½ teaspoon baking soda

1½ cups Cap'n Crunch cereal

PEANUT BUTTER WITH CAP'N CRUNCH COOKIES

MAKES: 20 to 24 cookies | **ACTIVE TIME:** 20 to 25 minutes

This is crunchy peanut butter, Coolhaus-style: the pleasant snap of Cap'n Crunch cereal, countered by smooth peanut butter cookies. Great in the morning, afternoon, or evening, and for a midnight snack. Also terrific with boozy flavors for a proper first meal of the day!

1 **Mix wets:** Place butter in a saucepan and set over low heat until just half is melted. Cool for 5 minutes.

2 Pour cooled butter into a large bowl. Add brown sugar and whisk to combine. Add peanut butter and whiskto combine. Whisk in egg and yolk, one at a time, then whisk in vanilla. Set aside.

3 **Mix dries:** In a small bowl, whisk together granulated sugar and cinnamon. Set aside.

4 In a medium bowl, whisk together flour, salt, and baking soda.

5 Add dries, one third at a time, to wets, mixing with a rubber spatula or wooden spoon to combine. Add cereal, mixing until evenly distributed. Be careful not to overmix or overcrush cereal.

6 Wrap bowl with plastic wrap and refrigerate for at least 20 minutes.

7 Preheat oven to 325 degrees, with racks in upper and lower thirds. Line two half-sheet baking pans with parchment paper.

8 Form dough into balls about the size of whole walnuts, roll in

reserved cinnamon-sugar mixture, and place 2 inches apart on prepared baking sheets.

9 Bake for 10 to 12 minutes, or until edges are light brown and centers are still wet—don't overbake.

10 Immediately transfer cookies to a cooling rack. Let cool for 1 hour before serving.

2 sticks (16 tablespoons) unsalted butter

S'MORES COOKIES

MAKES ABOUT: 24 cookies | **ACTIVE TIME:** 20 to 25 minutes

Never been a Girl Scout? This is what you missed out on—but now you can enjoy s'mores in the comfort of your own home without the threat of being attacked by a bear at a campsite. We bake these at a slightly higher heat than our other cookies so the marshmallows get nice and toasty, evoking that campfire char. Honey grahams and chocolate chips complete the sweet-and-roasty package.

1 **Mix wets:** Place butter in a saucepan and set over low heat until just half is melted. Cool for 5 minutes.

2 Pour cooled butter into a large bowl. Add both sugars and whisk to combine. Whisk in egg and yolk, one at a time, then whisk in vanilla. Set aside.

3 **Mix dries:** In a medium bowl, whisk together flour, salt, and baking soda.

4 Add dries, one third at a time, to wets, mixing with a rubber spatula or wooden spoon to combine. Fold in chocolate chips and crushed graham crackers until evenly distributed. Be careful not to overmix.

5 Wrap bowl with plastic wrap and refrigerate for at least 20 minutes.

6 Preheat oven to 350 degrees, with racks in upper and lower thirds. Line two half-sheet baking pans with parchment paper.

7 Form dough into balls about the size of whole walnuts and place 2 inches apart on prepared baking sheets. Place 1 marshmallow half on top of each cookie and gently press down.

8 Bake for 8 to 10 minutes, or until edges are light brown and marshmallows are toasty brown.

9 Immediately transfer cookies to a cooling rack. Let cool for 1 hour before serving.

2 sticks (16 tablespoons) unsalted butter

1 cup packed light brown sugar

1 cup packed dark brown sugar

1 large egg plus 1 large egg yolk

1½ teaspoons natural vanilla extract

2½ cups sifted pastry flour, or 2 cups sifted all-purpose flour plus ½ cup sifted cake flour (sift before measuring)

½ teaspoon kosher salt

½ teaspoon baking soda

1 cup semisweet chocolate chips (we like Guittard or Ghirardelli)

1½ cups crushed honey graham crackers (18 to 20 full-size crackers)

12 large marshmallows, halved

Ingredients

2 sticks (16 tablespoons) unsalted butter

1 cup packed light brown sugar

1 cup packed dark brown sugar

1 large egg plus 1 large egg yolk

1½ teaspoons natural vanilla extract

2½ cups sifted pastry flour, or 2 cups sifted all-purpose flour plus ½ cup sifted cake flour (sift before measuring)

½ teaspoon kosher salt

½ teaspoon baking soda

1 cup semisweet chocolate chips (we like Guittard or Ghirardelli)

⅔ cup lightly crushed salted pretzels

⅔ cup lightly crushed potato chips

⅔ cup cornflakes

SNACK FOOD CHOCOLATE CHIP COOKIES

MAKES: 20 to 24 cookies | **ACTIVE TIME:** 20 to 25 minutes

These cookies are for those moments when you can't decide whether to dig into a bag of chips, munch out on pretzels, break into some chocolate, or attack that late-night bowl of cereal.

1 **Mix wets:** Place butter in a saucepan and set over low heat, until just half is melted. Cool for 5 minutes.

2 Pour cooled butter into a large bowl. Add both sugars and whisk to combine. Whisk in eggs and yolk, one at a time, then whisk in vanilla.

3 **Mix dries:** In a medium bowl, whisk together flour, salt, and baking soda.

4 Add dries, one third at a time, to wets, mixing with a rubber spatula or wooden spoon to combine. Fold in chocolate chips, pretzels, potato chips, and cornflakes until evenly distributed. Be careful not to overmix or overcrush them.

5 Wrap bowl with plastic wrap and refrigerate for at least 20 minutes.

6 Preheat oven to 325 degrees, with racks in upper and lower thirds. Line two half-sheet baking pans with parchment paper.

7 Form dough into balls about the size of whole walnuts and place 2 inches apart on prepared baking sheets.

8 Bake for 10 to 12 minutes, or until edges are light brown and centers are still wet—don't overbake.

9 Immediately transfer cookies to a cooling rack. Let cool for 1 hour before serving.

VEGAN & GLUTEN-FREE

FOR COOKIES

1 cup canola oil

2 cups packed dark brown sugar

1 tablespoon orange juice

¼ teaspoon maple extract

1 teaspoon natural vanilla extract

2½ cups sifted pastry flour, or 2 cups sifted all-purpose flour plus ½ cup sifted cake flour (sift before measuring)

1 tablespoon ground cinnamon

1 teaspoon ground ginger

1 teaspoon ground nutmeg

½ teaspoon salt

½ teaspoon baking soda

½ teaspoon baking powder

1 cup shredded carrots (about 2 medium)

¾ cup old-fashioned rolled oats

¾ cup dried cranberries

VEGAN CARROT CAKE COOKIES

MAKES: 20 to 24 cookies | **ACTIVE TIME:** 20 to 25 minutes

You'll take to these cookies instantly. A burst of citrus from the orange enhances the carrots' natural sweetness, while cinnamon and nutmeg add personality to every bite. Bring some ginger into the mix, and you've got a vegan-style spice party in your mouth.

MAKE COOKIES

1 **Mix wets:** In a large bowl, whisk together oil and sugar to combine. Add orange juice, maple extract, and vanilla, and mix. Set aside.

2 **Mix dries:** In a medium bowl, whisk together flour, cinnamon, ginger, nutmeg, salt, baking soda, and baking powder.

3 Add dries, one third at a time, to wets, mixing with a rubber spatula or wooden spoon to combine. Fold in carrots, oats, and cranberries.

4 Wrap bowl with plastic wrap and refrigerate for at least 20 minutes.

5 Preheat oven to 325 degrees, with racks in lower and upper thirds. Line two half-sheet baking pans with parchment paper.

6 Form dough into balls about the size of whole walnuts and place 2 inches apart on prepared baking sheets.

7 Bake for 12 to 14 minutes, or until edges are light brown and centers are still wet—don't overbake.

8 Immediately transfer cookies to a cooling rack. Let cool for 1 hour before serving.

MEANWHILE, MAKE ICING

9 Using a stand or hand mixer on medium-high, beat margarine and cream cheese together until smooth and fluffy, 2 to 3 minutes.

10 Starting on low speed and working up to high, beat in powdered sugar and vanilla.

11 Using a pastry bag or a zip-top bag with one corner snipped, ice cooled cookies in a pattern of your liking and serve.

FOR ICING

1 stick (8 tablespoons) margarine or Earth Balance Natural Buttery Spread

1 cup vegan cream cheese (such as Tofutti), at room temperature

2 cups sifted powdered sugar (sift before measuring)

1 teaspoon natural vanilla extract

2 cups sweetened shredded coconut

¾ cup sliced almonds, with skins

2 sticks (16 tablespoons) unsalted butter

1 cup packed light brown sugar

1 cup granulated sugar

1 large egg plus 1 large egg yolk

1½ teaspoons natural vanilla extract

2½ cups almond meal flour

½ teaspoon salt

½ teaspoon baking soda

½ teaspoon baking powder

1 cup semisweet chocolate chips (we like Guittard or Ghirardelli)

TIP:

You can find almond meal flour in health food stores.

GLUTEN-FREE COCONUT ALMOND CHOCOLATE CHIP COOKIES

MAKES: 20 to 24 cookies | **ACTIVE TIME:** 20 to 25 minutes

Toasting the coconut and almonds brings out their soothingly sweet undertones.

1 Preheat oven to 325 degrees. Spread coconut and almonds on a baking sheet and toast in oven for 5 to 7 minutes, or until light brown. Set aside. Turn off oven.

2 **Mix wets:** Place butter in a saucepan and set over low heat until just half is melted. Cool for 5 minutes.

3 Pour cooled butter into a large bowl. Add sugars and whisk to combine. Whisk in egg and yolk, one at a time, then whisk in vanilla. Set aside.

4 **Mix dries:** In a medium bowl, whisk together almond flour, salt, baking soda, and baking powder.

5 Add dries, one third at a time, to wets, mixing with a rubber spatula or wooden spoon to combine. Fold in chocolate chips and toasted coconut and almonds until evenly distributed.

6 Wrap bowl with plastic wrap and refrigerate for at least 20 minutes.

7 Preheat oven to 325 degrees, with racks in upper and lower thirds of oven. Line two half-sheet baking pans with parchment paper.

8 Form dough into balls about the size of whole walnuts and place 2 inches apart on prepared baking sheets.

9 Bake for 12 to 14 minutes, or until edges are light brown and centers are still wet—don't overbake.

10 Transfer cookies to a cooling rack. Let cool for 1 hour before serving.

VEGAN GINGER MOLASSES COOKIES

MAKES: 20 to 24 cookies | **ACTIVE TIME:** 20 to 25 minutes

There's something so beautifully Asian about this flavor—it's like drinking a lovely ginger tea and drizzling a brown-sugary syrup in the cup instead of just using sugar.

1 **Mix wets:** In a bowl, using a hand mixer, mix together vegan spread and sugar until just creamy, 1 to 2 minutes. Add molasses, flaxseed mixture, and white vinegar and mix to combine. Set aside.

2 **Mix dries:** In a medium bowl, whisk together bread flour, baking soda, ginger, cinnamon, cloves, and cardamom.

3 Add dries, one third at a time, to wets, mixing with a rubber spatula or wooden spoon to combine.

4 Wrap bowl with plastic wrap and refrigerate for at least 20 minutes.

5 Preheat oven to 325 degrees, with racks in lower and upper thirds. Line two half-sheet baking pans with parchment paper.

6 Form dough into balls about the size of whole walnuts and place 2 inches apart on prepared baking sheets.

7 Bake for 8 to 10 minutes, or until edges are light brown and centers are still wet—don't overbake.

8 Immediately transfer cookies to a cooling rack. Let cool for 1 hour before serving.

1 stick (8 tablespoons) Earth Balance Natural Buttery Spread

2 cups granulated sugar

½ cup molasses

2 tablespoons flaxseeds pureed with 6 tablespoons water

1 tablespoon white vinegar

2½ cups sifted bread flour (sift before measuring)

1 tablespoon baking soda

2 teaspoons ground ginger

½ teaspoon ground cinnamon

½ teaspoon ground cloves

½ teaspoon ground cardamom

MAKE YOUR OWN

On August 17, 2012, at City Hall in Manhattan, we officially tied the knot. Then one month later, on September 15, we unofficially wed again (bicoastally, just like our business) in Los Angeles. Both occasions were overflowing with joy, love, and support and were so amazingly fun and magical that we'd have a wedding every month if we could. But what really took the cake was our Coolhaus Wedding Cake: a four-tiered sculpture of massive ice cream sandwiches for everyone to feast on. (Bottom tier: Oatmeal Raisin Cookie and Baked Apple Ice Cream; second tier: Vegan Ginger Molasses Cookie and Meyer Lemon Gelato; third tier: Double Chocolate Cookie and Dirty Mint Chip Ice Cream; top tier: Chocolate Chip Cookie and Tahitian Vanilla Bean Ice Cream.)

We both wore white summery dresses—Natasha went mod-style with crazy, Bauhaus-looking shoes. Freya wore a glammy dress she picked up in Paris.

The City Hall ceremony was intimate—just close family and friends, then we celebrated at one of our favorite restaurants, Vanessa's Dumpling House in Williamsburg, Brooklyn. We were almost late to our own party because our cab driver didn't know how to get there and wouldn't go the "extra mile" to deliver two brides to their wedding day celebration! He left us and our two friends carrying all the gin and bourbon punch ingredients on our heads on the Bowery. We had to hitch another cab to get across the river.

The L.A. ceremony was at Natasha's parents' house and featured tequila bars and tacos—the perfect street-food answer to New York City's dumplings.

We're excited to share this recipe, because for us, our wedding was a celebration not only of our relationship but also of what we have achieved at Coolhaus.

EQUIPMENT:

Two 8-inch round cake pans, 2 to 3 inches deep

One acetate food-safe cake strip (also called a "cake band"), or parchment paper, cut into a 3-by-14-inch strip

Ice cream scoop

Rubber spatula

1 recipe cookie dough of your choice

1 recipe ice cream of your choice

COOLHAUS ICE CREAM SANDWICH CAKE

MAKES: One 8-inch cake; serves 6 to 8 | **ACTIVE TIME:** 1 hour 25 minutes

1 Preheat oven to 325 degrees, with racks in upper and lower thirds. Coat cake pans with nonstick cooking spray.

2 Place half of cookie dough into each pan and press down to spread evenly.

3 Bake for 25 minutes, or until edges are golden and center puffs up and no longer looks wet.

4 Remove from oven and let cool for 30 minutes.

5 When completely cool, run a knife around edges and invert pans, tapping bottom of pans and shaking cookies out onto work surface.

6 Remove ice cream from freezer and let soften, 5 to 10 minutes.

7 Wipe 1 pan clean. Line interior circumference of pan with acetate cake strip or parchment paper strip.

8 Fit 1 cookie into bottom of pan. Use an ice cream scoop and a rubber spatula to spread softened ice cream on top of cookie in pan.

9 Top with remaining cookie, pressing it gently into ice cream to close any gaps and force out any air bubbles.

10 Immediately place in freezer and freeze for at least 4 hours.

11 Shake cake out of pan. Peel away cake strip before serving.

COOLHAUS MINI ICE CREAM SANDWICHES

MAKES ABOUT: 2 dozen mini ice cream sandwiches | **ACTIVE TIME:** 10 minutes

Everyone asks for mini ice cream sandwiches in our stores and at our trucks. We get the most inquiries from parents, especially for kids' parties. In the interest of giving the people what they want, we started a promotion with Girl Scout Cookies, pairing our ice creams with Samoas, Thin Mints, and Tagalongs and selling them three at a time. They were a big (mini!) hit.

1   Preheat oven to 325 degrees with a rack in the middle. Line a half-sheet baking pan with parchment paper.

2   Using 2 teaspoons of dough for each cookie, make balls of dough. Set balls 1 inch apart on prepared baking sheet.

3   Bake for 8 minutes, or until edges begin to brown. Transfer to a cooling rack to cool.

4   When cookies are completely cool, place 1 tablespoon ice cream on top of 1 cookie. Top with a second cookie, pressing down gently. Freeze for at least 15 minutes before serving.

1 recipe cookie dough of your choice (for recipes containing chocolate chips, use minis)

1 recipe ice cream of your choice (for recipes containing chocolate chips, use minis)

SHAKES, DRINKS, TOPPINGS & OTHER TREATS

HOT CHOCOLATE

MAKES: 1 quart | **ACTIVE TIME:** 20 minutes

1 In a medium saucepan, heat milk and half-and-half over medium heat just until boiling.

2 Add both chocolates to hot milk mixture and whisk until smooth. Remove from heat and whisk in sugar and espresso. Mix until combined.

3 Serve topped with Marshies or whipped cream, if desired.

2½ cups whole milk

2 cups half-and-half

4 ounces bittersweet chocolate (64% to 72% cacao), chopped

4 ounces milk chocolate, chopped

1 tablespoon granulated sugar

1 teaspoon espresso powder

Marshies (page 226) or Whipped Cream (optional)

WHIPPED CREAM

MAKES ABOUT: 2 cups | **ACTIVE TIME:** 3 minutes

In the bowl of a stand mixer fitted with the whisk attachment, or using a hand mixer, whip cream on medium-high speed until it forms stiff peaks. Beat in sugar and vanilla and mix for 1 minute more. Serve immediately.

1 cup heavy cream

1 tablespoon granulated sugar

1 teaspoon natural vanilla extract

MARSHIES

MAKES ABOUT: 1 half-sheet pan | **ACTIVE TIME:** 30 minutes

Terrific with our Hot Chocolate.

2 tablespoons plus 1 teaspoon unflavored gelatin

1¾ cups granulated sugar

⅔ cup light corn syrup

7 large egg whites, at room temperature

½ teaspoon salt

4 teaspoons natural vanilla extract

1 cup cornstarch

1 cup sifted powdered sugar

1 Dissolve gelatin in 1 cup cold water. Set aside.

2 In a small saucepan, heat granulated sugar, corn syrup, and ⅔ cup cold water over medium-high heat until it registers 245 degrees on a candy thermometer, 10 to 12 minutes.

3 Meanwhile, in a large bowl, beat egg whites with a hand mixer on low speed until frothy, about 5 minutes. Add salt and increase mixer speed to medium. Beat whites until thick and fluffy, about 5 minutes.

4 When syrup in saucepan registers 245 degrees, with mixer running, slowly pour hot liquid into egg whites, avoiding beaters of your mixer.

5 Scrape gelatin mixture into same saucepan you used for syrup, stirring to dissolve. Pour gelatin into whites, with mixer running on medium-high speed, then add vanilla and beat for 10 minutes, or until mixture is completely cool.

6 In a small bowl, combine cornstarch and powdered sugar. Sift cornstarch mixture evenly over a half-sheet baking pan, leaving no bare spots. Use a spatula to spread gelatin–egg white mixture evenly over pan. Set aside to dry at room temperature for up to 4 hours or overnight.

7 Using a pizza cutter or scissors dusted with cornstarch, cut marshmallows into desired shape.

8 Store in airtight containers at room temperature for up to 1 week.

TIPS:

If you cook the syrup too long and the temperature goes over 245 degrees, don't worry! Just add a few tablespoons of water to cool it down.

If the marshmallows are too soft at the end, your candy thermometer is off. Calibrate it. It should read 212 degrees at sea level when dipped into boiling water.

If the bottom of the Marshies are wet, the whites were not beaten until completely cool. Dry by blotting with a paper towel, dust with the cornstarch mixture, and let dry for 24 hours.

ALTERNATE PREPARATION:

MARSHIE FLUFF Skip cutting the marshmallow into shapes and scoop it directly into an airtight container after drying. Store at room temperature.

BASIC COOLHAUS SHAKE

MAKES: one 16-ounce milkshake | **ACTIVE TIME:** 1 minute

At Coolhaus we're known for shaking things up . . . including milkshakes. Our signature ice cream shakes blend ice cream *and* cookies, so they are a creamy, crumbly dream come true. It's a great way to use cookies that are becoming stale, since moisture and whipping in the blender will reinvigorate them. The best part is you can get creative and mix and match any of our ice cream and cookie flavors. Custom-made combos are tons of fun. Just use the following recipe and insert your own flavors. Or choose one of our four favorites, opposite.

1   In a blender, combine ice cream, milk, and three quarters of cookie and blend on high for 30 seconds, until shake is pourable, but not too thick. (Use a bar spoon to loosen as needed.)

2   Pour into a serving glass. Top with whipped cream and remaining cookie.

1¼ cups ice cream of your choice

¼ cup whole milk

1 cookie of your choice, crumbled

Whipped cream (page 225)

OUR FAVORITE COMBOS:

Brown Butter Candied Bacon Ice Cream (page 126) + Snack Food Chocolate Chip Cookie (page 210)

Dirty Mint Chip Ice Cream (page 40) + Double Chocolate Cookie (page 188)

Nutella Toasted Almond Ice Cream + Red Velvet Cookie (page 204)

Salted Caramel Ice Cream (page 109) + Snickerdoodle Cookie (page 194)

2 cups hazelnuts

1½ pounds milk chocolate, chopped, or equal amount milk chocolate chips

6 tablespoons sifted powdered sugar

2 tablespoons unsweetened cocoa powder

1 teaspoon natural vanilla extract

6 tablespoons canola oil

1 teaspoon sea salt

TIP:

Don't store this spread in the fridge, or it will solidify. The mixture should be soft. If it hardens, microwave until soft.

CHOCOLATE HAZELNUT SPREAD

MAKES ABOUT: 1 quart | **ACTIVE TIME:** 30 to 40 minutes

This is terrific on toast and even better on ice cream. You can also use it as a dip for cookies.

1 Preheat oven to 200 degrees.

2 Place hazelnuts on a baking sheet and toast in oven until golden brown, about 10 minutes.

3 With a dry cloth, rub off skins while hazelnuts are hot (you may not be able to remove all skins); discard skins. Place hazelnuts in a small bowl.

4 Place chocolate in a metal bowl set over a saucepan of simmering water. Cook, stirring, until melted and smooth, about 6 minutes. Turn off heat and set aside over water bath.

5 Place half of hazelnuts into a food processor. Process until well ground, then add remaining hazelnuts and process until texture is like peanut butter.

6 Add melted chocolate, powdered sugar, cocoa, and vanilla to food processor, then slowly add oil. Process until combined and smooth. Add salt.

7 Scrape spread into an airtight quart-size container. Let cool at room temperature. Store at room temperature for up to 3 weeks.

FRIED CHICKEN CARAMEL

MAKES ABOUT: 2½ cups | **ACTIVE TIME:** 1 hour 50 minutes

Awesome as an ice cream topping! Serve over Tahitian Vanilla Bean (page 42), Brown Butter Candied Bacon (page 126), Beer & Pretzel (page 64), Kit Kat (page 98), Nutella Toasted Almond (page 101), Salted Caramel (page 109), and Salted Chocolate Almond Joy (page 112).

1   Warm a large heavy-bottomed pan over medium heat. Add chicken skin to dry pan. Add ½ teaspoon salt, a pinch of sage, a pinch of cayenne, and the black pepper and brown skin until deep golden, stirring and turning as needed, about 10 minutes.

2   Deglaze pan with chicken broth, scraping bottom of pan to loosen any browned bits.

3   Add remaining sage and bouillon cube and simmer for 30 minutes. Remove and discard chicken skin with a slotted spoon, leaving smaller bits in for flavor.

4   Add caramel, and simmer on low, stirring, for 30 minutes to infuse flavors. Add remaining ½ teaspoon salt, remaining pinch cayenne, and pepper to taste.

5   Remove from heat and pour into a bowl. Let cool and mix with immersion blender or hand mixer to emulsify. Caramel can be refrigerated in an airtight container for 1 month or frozen for up to 3 months.

3 ounces chicken skin, chopped (about ⅓ cup)

1 teaspoon kosher salt

¼ teaspoon dried sage

2 pinches cayenne pepper

½ teaspoon freshly ground black pepper, plus more as needed

1 cup chicken stock

½ cube chicken bouillon

2 cups store-bought caramel sauce (we like Trader Joe's Fleur de Sel Caramel Sauce or Hershey's Caramel Syrup)

2 vanilla bean pods, split

2 cups heavy cream

10 tablespoons unsalted butter, cut into ¼-inch pieces

1½ teaspoons Maldon sea salt or fleur de sel

Vegetable oil nonstick spray

2⅔ cups granulated sugar

½ cup light corn syrup

SALTED CARAMEL PIECES

MAKES ABOUT: 100 caramels **|** **ACTIVE TIME:** 1 hour 30 minutes

These salty, sugary candies are best eaten on their own.

1. Using tip of a paring knife, scrape out seeds from vanilla bean pods. Discard pods.

2. In a small saucepan, combine vanilla bean seeds, cream, butter, and 1 teaspoon of sea salt. Bring to a boil over medium heat, cover, remove from heat, and steep for 10 minutes.

3. Line an 8-inch square baking pan with aluminum foil coated with nonstick spray. Set aside.

4. In a 4-quart saucepan, combine sugar, corn syrup, and ½ cup water. Bring to a boil over high heat, frequently swirling pan (do not stir), until mixture is amber-colored and registers 350 degrees on a candy thermometer. (Stay with pan and watch to make sure mixture doesn't burn.)

5. Remove from heat and carefully stir in cream mixture; be careful, mixture will foam. Return mixture to stovetop, reduce heat to medium-high, and cook, stirring frequently, until caramel registers 248 degrees on candy thermometer, 3 to 5 minutes.

6. Carefully transfer caramel to prepared baking pan. Using a rubber spatula, smooth surface of caramel and let cool for 10 minutes. Sprinkle with remaining ½ teaspoon salt.

7. Let cool to room temperature before cutting into 1-by-½-inch squares with a cold knife. The caramels will keep in an airtight container at room temperature for up to 1 week.

BACON SALT

MAKES: 1 pound | **ACTIVE TIME:** 30 minutes

We sometimes use this in place of the salt in Chocolate Chip Cookies (page 187) or for breakfast seasoning (it's great on eggs).

1 In a large skillet, cook bacon, turning once, until dark and crispy.

2 Place bacon in a food processor or blender and grind or pulse until coarse.

3 Transfer bacon to a large mortar. Add pepper. Grind together with a pestle, while slowly adding salt until completely mixed.

4 Store in an airtight container in the refrigerator for up to 3 weeks.

8 (1-ounce) strips bacon

½ tablespoon freshly ground black pepper

1 cup kosher salt

A GUIDE TO CREATING YOUR OWN COOLHAUSIAN FLAVORS

Once you become a practiced hand with our recipes, you can make your own flavors. Here are some tips on how to choose your own adventure.

KNOW YOUR PALATE

Do you prefer sweet or savory? What are some of your favorite flavor combinations? Your choices should feature those elements. For example, Freya's palate sits on the savory end of the scale, so she enjoys a salty aspect to balance the sweetness in her favorite ice creams.

KEEP YOUR EYES, EARS, AND MOUTH OPEN

We're always finding inspiration at restaurants, whether from groundbreaking modernist chefs like Chicago's Grant Achatz or at an everyday meal. When we are dining at our favorite restaurants and we taste a dish with an amazing flavor combination, we begin to ask ourselves, how can we make this into an ice cream? While eating at a sushi bar, for example, we thought about the ginger and wasabi on our plates and their spicy/cool profiles. We thought about ginger snaps sandwiching wasabi ice cream. Then we took it a step further—what if that wasabi ice cream had a chocolate base? Voilà, a new Coolhaus sandwich was born.

THINK OF THE DRINK

A lot of our flavors are inspired by cocktails. Well-made cocktails have terrific flavor profiles. Think of your ice cream as a handcrafted cocktail and translate accordingly. Liquor, wine, and beer are good pairing components.

GO TO YOUR HAPPY PLACE

Things that put smiles on our faces: a catchy song, a brightly colored painting, a smoking barbecue, landscape design. Some of our favorite creations: Santigold Strawberry Ice Cream, Blood Orange & Cranberry Gelato, Chocolate Chipotle Barbecue Ice Cream, and Highlime Pie Ice Cream Sandwiches.

RELEASE YOUR INNER CHILD

Send your soul back to a simpler time. What were some of your favorite childhood indulgences? Peanut butter and jelly sandwiches? S'mores? Whipped pineapple drinks at Disneyland? Sugary cereals? All great ice cream material.

CONSIDER CELEBRATIONS

The sweet potato marshmallow casserole is an ever-present side dish at our family Thanksgivings. We also look forward to some rum-laced eggnog at Christmas and will belly up to the bar for a pint of Guinness and some salty pretzels on St. Patrick's Day. Who says you can't prolong these holidays on the dessert plate?

We have very few hard-and-fast rules in our ice cream making, but we find that these guidelines help.

1   If there's a salty or savory component in an ice cream, always counter it with some sweet. Peking Duck ice cream on its own? Not so much. But add some plum sauce and now we're talking!

2   Sometimes every element of an inspirational dish doesn't need to be included in a flavor. Our Balsamic Fig Mascarpone flavor was inspired by a cheese plate we made, which included some arugula. The flavor finally came together when we dropped the arugula.

3   While we're on the topic of cheese, stick to the mellow, young side of the spectrum, since stinky, aged cheeses tend to overwhelm. One of our biggest failures was a Waldorf salad ice cream, because of the blue cheese.

4   Which brings us to the most important tenet: If it doesn't sound appetizing as an ice cream, it probably isn't. Know when to move on.

Once you've hit inspiration, play with it and test the hell out of it. Have tasting parties. And when you're successful, don't forget to name it—for us, that's half the fun. But most important, dig in and enjoy!

Share your fantasy flavors with us at: Natasha@eatcoolhaus.com.

WHERE TO FIND COOLHAUS ICE CREAM SANDWICHES

ONLINE AND RETAIL

http://eatcoolhaus.com/store
Check your local gourmet grocer or natural foods store.

TRUCKS

Austin
Dallas
Los Angeles
New York City

SHOPS

Culver City, California
Pasadena, California

ACKNOWLEDGMENTS

Natasha and Freya would like to thank our friends and family for preliminary and caring caution on our Coolhaus journey and the utter, unwavering support once we launched and began to grow. Barbara and Geoff Case, for their pride and support of our unexpected career journey; Sarah Case, who will one day bring Coolhaus to France, along with all of the love and support of the Case and Dourmashkin extended family, including Caitlin Dourmashkin and Galen Summer, for their New York City hospitality, and Camille Dourmashkin, for her summertime scooping, and the Feldmans and our grandparents. Susana Reyes, for allowing us to test our original recipes in her kitchen and park our original truck in her driveway and for all the love and support through the years. Shannon, Jaimee, and Carissa Estreller, for their official and unofficial work at Coolhaus, along with all the *titas*. Sarah Lehrer-Graiwer and Jeff Hassay, who have gone with us to every Coachella since our launch, for listening to Coolhaus banters and hosting unofficial Farchitecture idea labs. Ari Heckman and Ethan Feirstein, who have been involved bicoastally at Coolhaus and hosted the first office site of our New York City launch. We look forward to saying "hello" to new business with you. Ronna Reed, for her incredible enthusiasm, energy, and knowledge, and her daughter, Justine Jones, for the culinary inspiration, and medium and little Morgan Jones for appearing in the background of Google hangouts now and again. Amber Hawkes and Daniel Lehrer-Graiwer, for their unwavering friendship; Erica Schwarzberg, for her official and unofficial Coolhaus P.R.; Carrie Foster, for concept design work; and Jen Leary, for magnetic fabric work. Rebecca Rudolph, Cathy Johnson, and Gitta Brema of Design, Bitches, for architectural and brand work. Peter Christensen, for his friendship and support and for making us laugh. The original Coachella gang, Patrick Maple, Sean Simbro, Kristen Gordon, Sophie Holt, and Alyssa Pitman. Amy Melin, for being the very first recipe tester; Katrina Mosher, for sending a link that inspired our edible wrappers; and Rhoi Carpena, for his support at Walt Disney Imagineering. The Stern-McCullaugh family, for their support at Coolhaus. All of our clients, customers, and fans. The generous and supportive food-writing world, for all the P.R. over the years. Katherine Latshaw and Frank Weimann, for believing in us, and Rux Martin and Houghton Mifflin Harcourt, for taking it to fruition. Family friends who have been inspirational in their respective creative fields: Brian Leatart, for a magical photography shoot; we look forward to many more; Penny De Los Santos, for her keen eye and sensibility to our vibe in her photos; our incredibly devoted, passionate, creative, and hardworking staff. Dan and Ashlee Fishman and Bobby Margolis, for the incredible partnership and mentoring. Kathleen Squires—we could not possibly have had more fun and found someone who really "got it" in terms of what we were going for with this book. Thank you for being a crusader with us on this project. It was the experience of a lifetime to author this book with you!

Kathleen would like to thank helpers, tasters, guinea pigs, giant supporters: John R. Squires, Catherine Squires, Christine Squires, Steven Pashkoff, Mary Lou Squires, John A. Squires, super-tester Elizabeth Squires, super-taster William Squires, my part-time dog, Riggins, Edna Laura Perez, Miguel Juan Rodriguez-Marxuach, Miguel J. Rodriguez-Perez, Laura E. Rodriguez-Perez, Ana Teresa Rodriguez-Perez, Canela Rodriguez-Perez, and Liam Rodriguez-Perez. My favorite writer comrades, Andrea Strong and Julie Besonen, for their well of friendship; testers, friends, great chefs Becky Morrison and Julie Carrion; tester/ helper Becky McGuigan at The Kitchen at Billings Forge; über-tester, critiquer, Google-chatter, and team Coolhaus mascot Ronna Reed; genius pastry chef David Baker; photography masterminds Brian Leatart and Penny De Los Santos; fan club president, ice cream eater, cookie monster, and unwavering fountain of love Hernan "Ronnie" Rodriguez; awesome agents Katherine Latshaw and Frank Weimann of the Literary Group International; extraordinary editor Rux Martin and the entire team at Houghton Mifflin Harcourt. Most especially, the brilliant brand builders and coolest collaborators ever Natasha Case and Freya Estreller—I wish I could write every book with the two of you.

NATASHA CASE (*left*) is a Los Angeles native. She attended UC Berkeley for undergraduate studies, where she majored in architecture and double minored in city and regional planning and Italian studies. Natasha furthered these studies at UCLA, where she pursued a master of architecture and, after graduating, worked as an architectural intern at Walt Disney Imagineering in hotel and master planning. During this time, she started baking cookies and making ice cream and naming the ice cream sandwich combinations after famous architects and architectural movements. She handed them out to her peers, who found them to be tasty comic relief in spite of recent layoffs and discussion of further impending cutbacks. She had also just met Freya, who was helping her make the product behind the scenes and was putting numbers to the concept as a business model. Natasha works today as the CEO of Coolhaus, creating new product opportunities, building new relationships, and innovating ideas that keep Coolhaus on top of its game as zealous expansion continues.

FREYA ESTRELLER (*right*) is cofounder and co-owner of Coolhaus. She was born and raised in Los Angeles, CA, and has a BA in sociology with a minor in business from Cornell University. Prior to founding Coolhaus, she worked in real estate development, design, and finance, helping to build and/or renovate more than three hundred housing units on the East and West Coasts. She currently splits her time between Los Angeles, New York City, and Austin (where all the trucks are!), has a mini schnauzer named Hamilton, whom she fiercely loves, and is thankful every day for getting to live her entrepreneurial dream.

KATHLEEN SQUIRES is a food writing veteran whose work has spanned book, blog, newsprint, and magazine. Her work has appeared in *Saveur*, the *Wall Street Journal*, *Cooking Light*, Zagat.com, *Gourmet, New York* magazine, *National Geographic Traveler*, *Real Simple*, *Budget Travel*, *Time Out New York*, the *New York Daily News*, the *New York Post*, the *New York Observer*, *Metro*, *Paper*, and many other publications. She lives in New York City.

INDEX